MESSAGES
& other stories

READ MORE BY THIS AUTHOR:
charlieweaverrolfe.com

Cover design © Charlie Weaver Rolfe
from artwork by Peggy Marlena Wilson

CWR Books
Brighton, UK

MESSAGES
& other stories

*Charlie
Weaver
Rolfe*

AUTHOR'S NOTE

Read these stories and they might change your life.

The author accepts no liability, however, for any stories which change your life in ways you are unhappy with and subsequently wish to reverse.

MESSAGES

The messages aren't just for me. So I don't feel special.

I feel – well, I do feel special, but just in the sense that I feel lucky. What I mean is, I don't feel special in the sense that I've been specially chosen because of anything special about me. It's just that I'm the one getting the messages, for whatever reason, not someone else. And it's not that I'm just getting one or two – I'm getting them constantly, all the time, a torrent of messages like I'm standing under a waterfall and I need to stand strong or I'll get swept away and I can't, I mustn't get swept away, because I need be here for my girlfriend.

About being special – as a kid sometimes I'd have the feeling that I was here on some sort of secret mission, not even my parents knew about it and not even my sister, who was older than me, and the secret mission was like my destiny, like in Dungeons and Dragons and all of that. But later I realised that all kids feel that and my secret mission had not developed in any clear way along the paths that I'd imagined it, and also I guess as I grew up the films and stories that must have inspired my secret mission had piled up so much on top of each other that they kind of lost their colour, if that makes sense, I mean lost their brightness. The same with songs that you listen to so many times, they just go flat. It might not happen until the hundredth time, but suddenly they've lost that thing and you might have to wait another ten years before they get it back again, that flavour, that feeling they used to have – or maybe they'll never get it back.

So I guess that's what happens to lots of kids – your secret mission stops feeling special, or stops being secret, and you grow up. Tell too many other people, kids or your parents or teachers at school, and your mission starts feeling like somebody else's, like the same mission as everyone else. Or maybe you just tell your sister and it makes it seem stupid like it always does.

And that's the thing. If the messages aren't just for me, there's nothing secret or special about the fact that it's me that's getting them. It's more like there's a radio, the way that radios used to be, where you tune into a frequency and either there's a radio station or you just get noise, a crackle or hiss, and just because you hear music playing, or the news, or a football commentary, you don't think – this is my secret mission, to hear this music, this news, this commentary. You just listen to it – or you don't. Maybe you search for another station. Only that's not the kind of radio that it is for me, I can't tune out, and sometimes I wonder how many people are tuned into the same station, how many of us under the waterfall, and I ask myself who's choosing the songs but I know there's no point asking that. There's no point asking that.

The point is – *I'm in communication*. After all these years. I guess I mean since I was still a kid, before all the stories and films and songs got so layered up inside my head that I couldn't make sense of anything, no music in the messages, no meaning, it was all just mush, like a bad school dinner from those huge steel vats – like a plate of the cabbage, boiled grey, that my sister used to hide in her pockets so her plate was clean for the dinner ladies.

My life was like a plate of cabbage, and all I could hear was cabbage-noise. Whereas now – it's the whole brass band.

My sister keeps ringing. I've stopped picking up. I just wish my girlfriend could hear it too. Then we could really be together and it wouldn't matter if we got swept away.

The sea is like a neon blanket.

The night is so quiet you can hear the stars.

"Please," I say. "Just come outside…"

TOMATOES

A young man and a young woman were introduced at a party. They got on well, became friends, and started seeing more and more of each other, until the young man had the idea that he might be in love with the young woman. He couldn't be sure, but he remembered from an earlier experience the way that it made him not want to eat food. He also felt sort of electrical, like if he touched something metal he'd get a shock.

"What should I do?" he asked his flatmate.

"Tell her," his flatmate shrugged.

So when they were saying goodbye one night on their way back from the cinema, the young man finally told the young woman how it was that he felt about her.

It was dark in the street. The young woman looked down at the pavement while the young man spoke, and was quiet for a second or two once he had finished. Then she told him that she was in love with someone else. "I really appreciate you as a friend," she said. "I hope we can stay friends – but I'm sorry…" She looked away.

The young man also looked down at the pavement.

"Do I know him?" he asked.

"No," said the young woman.

"Is he taller than me?"

"No," she said.

"What about arms? Are his longer than mine? Has he got special double-jointed limbs? Can he count to five hundred without pausing for breath? Does he speak Latin?" he asked.

"Not as far as I know," said the young woman, perplexed. "But what's that got to do with anything?"

The young man didn't answer this.

"Did you know I played the violin?" he said. "Well now you know: I play the violin. I've played violin every day except on seven days since I was six years old.

The young woman didn't know what to say, but felt that she ought to say something. "Oh," she said.

"Yes," said the young man. "And I grow tomatoes in my garden – huge tomatoes, in a greenhouse, and I don't use any pesticides. Did you know that?"

"No," she said.

"Well now you know: I grow tomatoes in my garden and I know how to play the violin."

They stared at each other.

"I probably ought to go," the young woman said. "I promised my flatmate I'd cook dinner…"

"I came fourth in a national competition for young violin players in my age-group," the young man shouted after her. "Fourth!"

A car drove past playing very loud music.

Damn, thought the young man, watching her leave. That didn't go how I planned it.

A few months later, the young man received a phone call from the young woman, inviting him to her wedding. She was getting married to the man whom she had said she was in love with – who was also, it turned out, in love with her. They were both in love with each other.

"Will you come?" the young woman asked.

"Of course," said the young man. "Great!"

Although when he stopped to think about it, he wasn't so sure that he wanted to go to the wedding of someone that he himself was probably still in love with. I'm going to look like an idiot, he thought. I'll have to borrow a suit that doesn't fit me properly, and there'll be canapés being passed around that I won't know which way round to eat. The young man saw this taking place and started to fear the worst.

But in the event the wedding was fine. The weather was good, the people friendly. The groom shook him warmly by the hand.

"Congratulations."

"Glad you could make it."

"My pleasure," said the young man.

It was all very civil and friendly and warm.

Then, during the ceremony, the young man saw that two of the bridesmaids were at least as attractive as the bride – and later that evening, drinking champagne, he found himself talking to one of them. She was studying to be a landscape architect, although she had always wanted to be a gymnast.

"But things don't turn out how you plan them," she giggled.

"No, they don't," the man agreed.

Next thing he knew they were sharing a taxi.

The following morning, while the young man was still half-asleep in bed, the bridesmaid had put on his dressing gown and was looking out of the window.

Suddenly she became strangely excited.

"Oh my God!" she said. "Look at those tomatoes!"

CAFÉ CON LECHE

A man walks into a bar, asks the barman: "I'm looking for my wife – I mean *a wife* – and also I need some goats." "No goats here," says the barman, "but we do serve lamb, and my daughter is recently divorced if you would be interested in meeting her? She can cook a bit but she's messy, I can't say otherwise, and sometimes you just have to let her do her thing or she gets in a sulk, a fury even – and then she'll just go and do it anyway, and blame you if it goes wrong. But on the inside, as her father, I can tell you that she's a good person – and honest, you won't find a more honest wife. She just needs a thoughtful, sensitive type who understands her, who loves and respects her, and lets her be the person she is. Just not *too* sensitive…" the barman reconsiders. "*Too* sensitive would not work either. But dreamy – I suppose that's what I mean. A dreamy man who loves her for *the person she might be*, and doesn't think too much about what she's actually like…" "She sounds like a wonderful woman," says the man, "and of course I would love to meet her. But really the goats are the most important. The goats are necessary to manage the land. Does your daughter, who is obviously a woman who knows her own mind, have any fixed opinions about animal husbandry?" He sees the barman hesitate. "What I mean is, do you think she would clash with the goats?"

Okay, yes, let's go with that. That's the story.

Now go in.

Always too dark in these places and you have to make a split-second decision – leave? stay? – but ten more seconds and the choice is made, you're staying, you might want to change your mind – your eyes have had time to adjust to the light – but you're staying, I'm staying, so go to the bar. No barman but in this sort of place you go to the bar, they don't wait tables, which is why the Spaniards are up on stools, all men, all smoking, all fifty or sixty, even the ones who are only thirty, or else getting on for a hundred-and-five, and beyond them a kitchen with an oil-stained curtain pulled three-quarters across the doorway, a light and sizzling from within, a woman's voice, a man disputing, a television with football highlights that half the men stare upwards at, through their smoke, while the others read football newspapers, I could leave, still, they haven't seen me, I mean they haven't looked at me – but no, I'm staying, a girl comes out, "*Sí?*" she shouts. "Hello," I say, except in Spanish, "*Hola – pónme un café con leche, por favor…*"

Go outside again, sit down. Plastic chairs, plastic tables, slanting cobbled streets – the sun. So many days of rain but now it's sunshine, harsh and bright, the sandstone, or whatever stone it is, and every building painted white, you're blind, I'm blind beyond the parasol, a circle of shade in which I sit, studying the stubby brown bottle of San Miguel left on the corner of the table. Here she comes with my *café con leche*. "*Gracias.*" "*De nada,*" she says.

I always like this phrase, "It's nothing" – much less fraught than our alternatives, "No problem" (but there might have been),"My pleasure" (are you sure?). I like this country, I like these people,

17

they're not like me, perhaps that's why.

"Excuse me," I say, also in Spanish, "A question. I want to buy some goats…" The girl laughs, like I'm someone wonderful. And she's beautiful. This is unexpected. Not that she's beautiful, that's what they are, but that she laughs like I'm someone wonderful. "And also," I carry on now I've started, "I want to marry someone – *quiero casarme con alguien*." "Ah," she says, laughing, "*Ya entiendo* – a wife to help take care of the goats…" "No," I say, "The goats are – how you say? – the goats are *auto-suficientes*. The goats are to look after the garden…" I'm grinning, squinting up at her, an edge of sun shooting under the parasol, "The wife," I say, "is to look after me…" She smiles. "And who do you look after?"

Yes. Good question. The real, if not the only question. Yes, I could love this woman – this shimmering, modern-rustic goddess – and not just in the way that I love her already, which perhaps – who knows? – lacks permanence…

Okay, so let's think about it…

"You cook," I say, "And I wash up? The goats eat the garden. In the mornings, or else in the afternoons, you can still come and help out in the kitchen – if you want to – I know it's your father's bar… I'll stay at home and make sure the goats don't escape." "Wait," says the goddess, "*Espera un momento.* I have to go back inside…"

Sit in my shade, put a sugar in my coffee, sip it, shut my eyes and smile. I can see us, up in my white brick shack I have crazily brought with my great-uncle's legacy – crazily? or not so crazily? – the goats are grooming the field outside, she's standing with her back to me, washing up – I must have cooked this time – but no, no need to get bogged down in detail. The point is that I'm happy here, in the low evening sun of my fantasy – and so is my goddess, she's always laughing. The goats munch contentedly. Birds chirrup, the sun sets. And throughout the mornings and afternoons, whenever she isn't at work in the bar, the soft but constant threat of sex – and maybe even children? No. In time perhaps but no, not yet… The goats are the most important thing.

Perhaps she'll grow some vegetables?

Another sugar in my coffee. Another sip. Eyes closed again. And then, of course, the same old thought: "You're wasting your life with these fantasies, you're wasting your life in this mountain slum, this slow, sunlit Andalucian homage to a past that wasn't, a present that isn't, and a future – *mañana!* – that can't, or won't, with wrinkled old women in jacket and blouse and walking sticks scaling cobbled streets, and hens, a festival of hens that squawk all day but you never see, as the men hide out in the dark of bars – *mañana!* – drinking red wine for breakfast…" Is there something wrong with that? Really? But anyway that's the thought I have: "You're wasting your life with these fantasies, you're wasting my life, I'm wasting yours – whatever. And in the end – *so what?*"

The girl returns with a bowl of olives. I don't want olives with my coffee. No Spaniard would ever eat olives with coffee – but no, the olives aren't for me. The girl sits at the next table, between the next table and mine, picks up the stubby San Miguel I had assumed to have been another customer's, swigs it, and starts to consume the olives in a methodical, almost philosophical manner, looking out across the valley, chewing, and then removing the stones one by one and arranging them on the table – not on the next table, on mine – as if she were planning a line of houses, then a street, then a small community, with a crescent, a cul de sac, a winding path up into the hills – I've never seen a female eat so many olives in one sitting, she's almost at the end of the bowl and only a minute or so has passed – an urgent, and highly efficient philosophy, in fact a business, an industry. You can see how they built so much on the coast… She is beautiful, yes. Nothing sexual, nor erotic, but a form of pornography nonetheless, and designed especially for me, for a man with my peculiar fantasies of women, fierce, untamed yet domesticated, often if not always shouting, beating at dusty rugs with branches whilst accusing the goats of all kinds of crimes, of the wildest, most far-fetched misdemeanours…

The last stone moves into the village – and at once the village is swept from the table, razed, one palm sweeping them into the other and from there back into the bowl. She swigs the last of her San Miguel and puts this on its side in the bowl as well. Then she turns to look at me.

"I would have to speak with my father," she says, speaking in English now. "I marry an English once before *y*… not so good," she says. "*Cómo?*" – it's not that I didn't hear her, I'd just rather she only spoke in Spanish, preferably not a word of English, just an exasperated semi-tolerance falling some way short of understanding, a loyalty and some kind of trust – if not love then trust – based on this mutual misapprehension. "*Mi padre*… I marry an English before and now… and now where is he?"

I see. Once more, the real question. "*Desaparecido?*"

"Yes," she says. "*En marzo*. He went to buy some cheese."

I nod, drink some more of my coffee, think. This "English" could be a hard act to follow. Such clarity of purpose. Such ruthlessness in the pursuit of the object of desire – in this case, according to our goddess, cheese, which perhaps, no doubt, he is eating now, his most favoured, craved-for and coveted cheese, consuming his cheese in a fever of gluttony even as I move in on his ex… Or maybe he's eating olives. Yes. My coffee is finished, I'd like some olives, to go with the goats and the vegetables, the ones that the goats haven't decimated, and to go with lemon trees, I want citrus fruit – and also it needs to be next year already so that last year's olives are ready now. I sip once more from my empty cup. "I'm sorry about your husband. That's very difficult," – all of this in Spanish – "Would it be possible to have some olives?"

"*Claro,*" says my jilted goddess. "But first we go inside. Now you must talk to my father…"

The high smoke, low murmur, anaemic light and large-tiled floor, with cigarette butts and scrunched napkins and ripped-up sugar sachets and sweet wrappers, the wooden tables with stand-up menus, the seated men on stools at the bar and *las noticías* on the television – an earthquake in Chile, or Pakistan, or one of the places where earthquakes happen. China, maybe. Faraway.

"*Siéntese,*" my future wife, *mi amor* points at a chair, and really is there a finer pleasure than to be ordered about by a female of the Spanish persuasion, preferably a goddess, and even more so if there's food involved, *queso, jamón, pan* – olives.

"*Papá!*" she shouts into the kitchen, "*Ponme unas aceitunas* – and please, I want you to meet my friend. He is… *inglés*…" The men, their denim or dark-trousered knees up high, smoking, watching football and earthquakes, complementary forms of catastrophe, don't even turn to look. It's hard to imagine them anywhere but here or in a bar just like it, in another village the same as this one – or perhaps in the bar across the street. The second *inglés* of the barman's daughter is of no consequence one way or the other. Perhaps the same is true for the barman, who has not emerged. "*Papá!*" My maybe-wife enters the kitchen…

Olives!

The father of the bride appears from beyond the curtain in his traditional peasant-barman uniform with extra stains from kitchen-work – these jumpers! was there just one kind? were they requisitioned under Franco and given to men of a certain age? – with a second bowl, an ample portion, which he places on the bar. "*Papá,*" his daughter begins again, a differently coercive approach, and gesturing just minimally in my direction she begins to remonstrate in daughterly tones, admonishing him, before finally coaxing him out from behind his ugly granite bar-defences – his expression unchanged throughout, a heroic image of resignation – and over to sit down at what is now our table. The bowl of olives travels with him and is placed in the middle.

"*Sí?*" he says loudly, getting right to the point.

"*Encantado,*" I say. We shake hands.

"*Papá,*" says our go-between, almost sweetly, "*me voy a casar con este hombre* – I'm going to marry him." She glances at me only briefly, while I wait to start on the *aceitunas.*

"*Vale, vale, vale,*" says my father-in-law. "*Como tu quieras* – whatever you like."

"*Gracias, papá! – gracias!*" She hugs him – and over his shoulder, not-so-surreptitiously smiles at me.

I smile back – and permit myself an olive.

"*Una cerveza?*" the barman asks me, once released.

"Yes please," I say gratefully. "*Muchas gracias!*"

He stands and returns behind the bar, pulls me *una caña* and tells the men: "*Mi hija se va a casar con ese muchacho ahí sentado…*"

"*Muy bien, muy bien!*" the men raise their glasses, to him, to me, "*Enhorabuena* – congratulations!"

"*Gracias,*" I raise a hand, like the Queen.

My soon-to-be wife has started eating the olives, her second bowl, with the same focus and efficiency as she emptied the first. Her father brings me my *cerveza* and puts in front of me without breaking his stride. "*Muchas gracias,*" I say again.

"He likes you," says my goddess, who is not quite as beautiful in a dingy bar as she is silhouetted by the late morning sun, but is beautiful enough for me.

"He's very nice," I say in Spanish – "*Es muy simpático.*"

"Yes," she nods, removing a stone from her lips, adding it to a crescent curving out from the existing settlement. "But he is worried because of my last husband…"

"*Claro,*" I nod, show empathy. "*Desde luego.*"

"He asks me, What if he leaves for cheese?"

I eat more olives before she consumes the whole bowl herself.

"*Entiendo,*" I shrug.

Yes, I understand. We have reached the marriage vows. Eat an olive, remove the stone, set to work building my own small village to show I am also a serious person – although it may always be smaller than hers, I can't eat olives with the same dedication. "Like your former husband, I also like cheese…" – good to be honest when possible – "but I am not the same man. Your former husband…" I shake my head. As I do not know her former husband I am unable to say much more. We are English, it may be that we're similar. I watch her olive-stone village grow at a rate I know I will never match. "Your former husband… was another man." Best to leave it there.

Eat some olives, build my village. My wife-to-be is back in the kitchen and remonstrating with her father again, updating him on my firmish intentions. I have some time to think about things, to consider my unexpected progress. I look around.

At a table in the back of the café, wedged between the entrance to *los aseos* and a cigarette machine, a boy of about eight years old sits staring at the smaller patterned tiles on the wall. No other women around. To whom does this boy pertain?

Eat more olives, eat more olives – *faster! faster! build! build!* – if my goddess tells me this boy is her child I may choke on an olive and require urgent assistance, an ambulance bouncing wildly up winding cobbled streets in vain. And just as I'm considering this, she pulls back the oil-stained curtain once more, exits the kitchen, returns to our table, sits and turns to follow my gaze so that both of us now are watching the boy.

The boy continues to stare at the tiles, oblivious not only to our attention but it seems to everything else as well. Of course she is the boy's mother – and the "English" who left for cheese, her former husband, is the father…

I look to her, enquiring.

"Jim," she tells me. "*Mi hijo,* Jim. My son," she smiles.

They have named their Spanglish offspring Jim. Their abandoned, or half-abandoned, child, perhaps autistic, but at any rate obsessed with tiles and lacking interest in the outside world, except in small and manageable, repetitively patterned sections. Keep him away from the cobbled streets. Don't let him look at trees!

But – I haven't choked on an olive.

And pregnancy, to be pragmatic, is a very long and arduous process, three parts boredom to one anxiety, there are few if any other purposes to which a person would sacrifice such time, such energy – *and their entire body* – without the extreme coercion of others. Or indeed, if a man were expected to do it, the full apparatus of a totalitarian state… This boy, this Jim, already exists.

He is born and will presumably now grow by himself. He appears not to have any further physical disabilities. If I were also "to leave for cheese" no doubt my wife would continue to blame her previous husband, at least predominantly, whilst forming a picture, a little skewed, of the English male in general. Fond of cheese – and unreliable.

"*Autístico?*" I ask her.

"*Cómo?*" she says.

"*Nada,*" I shake my head. "*Nada.*"

So yes. We are down to brass tacks. Now let's see just how fickle I am… The boy is apparently "*tímido*" – not autistic. We'll see. I don't imagine this village to be the first place to go for a diagnosis, whatever was wrong with you. Look at me. But you have to take the positives. The boy's grandfather has accepted the match, and I can't imagine a better in-law – a brusque, straightforward, seventy-percent-silent/thirty-percent-shouting type, and with his own bar and supply of olives, not to mention *cerveza* and *café con leche*. His world is one of oil-stains and cigarette smoke and foot-ball highlights. Every so often he sweeps the floor – unless he gets his daughter to do it. Mother-in-law? Deceased, I assume. And so he accepts his daughter's wishes. A widower, a pragmatist, a man of the soil. In a sense, a kind of human goat, tending to his café-garden…

My almost-wife is telling me that her grandmother also wishes to meet me – and of course I would love to meet her too, I always get on well with grandmothers (they are mothers, but not so *emphatically*). I hope she's of that tiny kind, all elegant wrinkled determination, a saint – a survivor of the Civil War, *la dictadura*, and of so many subsequent chops and changes that it's hard to know, as an *extranjero*, which if any made any difference – and yet the most elderly seem to simply *endure*, climbing, always steadily climbing, in black skirt and shoes up cobbled streets, backed by a choir of hens.

"*Abuela!*" my goddess waves ecstatically, at once returned to her happy childhood and memories of – but wait… *who is this woman?* I was imagining one-hundred-and-five, but she can't be very much more than sixty. Stern. Spectacles. Marching towards me – an assassin from a parallel universe where lady-gangsters occupy smoky bars, deciding whether and who to kill, while their complicitly unknowing husbands raise kids, keep house, spend all the money, and try not to walk into the wrong room at parties. Two metres inside the stone doorway, she stops on the outer edge of the interior gloom, framed by the light, with one hand held behind her back, this *abuela* is in fact some way beyond elegant – she is, more accurately, severe. She also appears already to know the scene which she is now surveying, from a short distance, not yet wishing to enter. *Abuela* does not return my wave.

Two things happen quickly at once. My maybe-fiancé leaps from the table and rushes towards her grandmother. And no doubt due to my being startled by this, an olive, only minimally chewed, lodges itself in my windpipe – *I'm choking!*

No one else has noticed yet, I still have some air in my lungs, but my panic is swiftly depleting it. Maybe I have thirty seconds in which either to survive or to die, with a fair chance (if the former) that neither *abuela* nor her granddaughter need ever how close we came to the abrupt cancellation of our matrimony.

In any case, there is the time to realise that what I am experiencing is a near-death experience, during which I see with clarity that my whole life up until this point, with the exception of my "early years" (which I take to be until the age of seven) has been a more or less comprehensive waste of time. There are a couple of other, later moments that also present themselves as *conceivably meaningful*, but only as instances of the path not taken – as exceptions to the rule. I can't pretend that these isolated examples are in any way reflective of the person I am or in any way serve to legitimize the person that I have *chosen to be*.

So much for the mental aspect of my near-death experience. There is, of course, also a physical aspect involving a far-too-discreet attempt to dislodge the olive by coughing and banging my chest with my fist, the breakneck exploitation of oxygen by my increasingly frantic body, intense pressure on the brain, a hotness and synaesthetic redness of face that I can both see and feel, and the sudden decision to lurch and stand at the same time as trying to kneel – the exact moment at which, *deus ex machina*, the thick strong arms of a miraculous Heimlich are around my midriff, there follows a quick and powerful squeeze, a pang of acute embarrass-ment, and – as if it had never resisted – the olive shooting out from my throat and ricocheting against the wall.

My near-death experience thus concluded, I stoop, my clammy hands on my knees, to suck in the air, once, twice, whilst examin-ing the irregular texture of the large floor-tiles in further detail. They're grey but yes, there's more to it than that…

Meanwhile Heimlich – one of the standard-issue, Franco-era, taciturn Spanish men at the bar – has returned to his regular stool so quickly that I'm not even sure which one he was. They sit watch-ing the female presenter enthuse about whatever's coming next, almost certainly either more *noticias* or football highlights or both. No one shows any interest in my recent calamity – which includes my goddess and her grandmother, both of whom are looking at me although not with any particular expression of concern. I assume they only saw the end of it, alerted by the departing olive.

They resume their conversation, my betrothed talking animatedly while *abuela* remains silent, now in profile, so I'm able to see her previously hidden left-hand as it clenches and unclenches at regular intervals behind her back – the exact mannerism of a cinema Nazi, or perhaps ex-Nazi, now respectably living out their twilight years in South America. She doesn't show any sign of joy at the news she is receiving, but it's also possible that signs of joy are not part of her repertoire and in fact she is euphoric.

I wave again.

Abuela nods.

She is hugged by her granddaughter.

She leaves.

My fiancé, sitting beside me once more, is emotional. Tearful, even. I would love to have another *cerveza* but it's clearly not the moment to ask.

"*Mi abuela*," says my wife, beaming, "she likes you very much. She says you are a good man, she can see… that you are a good man. And *mi abuela* knows men. She is happy, very happy, that I will be married – with *a good man*…"

I wonder if *abuela* met the man before me?

We sit and talk. Get to know one another. Another beer arrives, one for each of us, and a third bowl of olives. I exercise caution, but my wife-to-be proceeds with her usual rigour, building and razing villages as we converse in a somewhat less action-packed fashion. I'm drunk now, due to lack of food, so I eat some of the crispy chips drenched in meaty oil that has also arrived.

Good. I could live on meaty oil. For a while.

In any case, the more I consider it, the surer I am that *abuela*, if she formed any judgement at all, almost certainly *did not like me*. If she had said "*buen hombre*" I would have heard her, surely? – at least if it was after I had finished choking. So either *mi amor* has wilfully misread her grandmother's feelings – or her absence of feelings – or else she's lying.

Again, good. Reassuring. We're back in a world I believe I'm familiar with, a world in which everyone either lies or else wilfully misreads everyone else, at every moment and in every way, and I lie too, but truthfully – I'm convinced that I only lie truthfully – the most truthful liar – the most eager misreader – and always – especially – perhaps exclusively – *to myself…*

And suddenly, God knows why, I find myself plunged into the warmest feelings of empathy towards my autistic adopted son, Jim, the solitary offspring of my rival and enabler – *my benefactor?* – my wife-to-be's previous Englishman, whose name I have not been told. Assuming of course that he *is* the solitary offspring… But really, this far in, does it matter? I must speak to her about this man *who left for cheese*, about our possible similarities, while also reassuring her as to the differences. I have no right but intoxication to be thinking of attempting this – but intoxication will do.

"*Tu hijo* – Jim," I begin, "– *su padre… Es que el queso – el deseo por el queso…*" Start again. "*Yo soy un hombre con deseos también,*" I say. "*Cada hombre… cada hombre tiene sus deseos – sus sueños – pero tu hijo…*" I shake my head, concentrating. "*Lo más importante es que una persona encuentra su felicidad a su manera, a su propia manera…*" I'm beating my chest with my fist – a learnt behaviour from my recent choking. The man in me is at issue here, nothing more nor less than that.

"*Yo, por ejemplo,*" – this is the crux of it – "*Yo, por ejemplo, quiero tener cábras… Ahora somos una familia, y yo quiero tener cabras…*"

I assume that she can't have understood much of this talk of men and desire, of men and cheese – but about the *cabras* she is clear. "Goats…" she says, shaking her head. "Goats is always problem." She taps her temple with two fingers. "*Son muy cabezonas…*"

Stubborn. Yes, goats are stubborn, she's right. And so, I am fully aware, is she – *muy cabezona*. They say that it takes one to know one but in this case I'm not sure that's necessary – just watch her eat olives. I only wish she could speak my language with the exquisite confusion I summon to hers! My fiancée and – who knows? – perhaps one day my wife, given time to develop her linguistic skills, sprawling an English of such unstructured complexity I can understand barely a word of it – and yet answer in the mangled Spanish of my deepest beliefs! And what degree of stubbornness, not to mention speech and language difficulties, to expect from our poor autistic son! The nobility of his suffering! In whatever sensory form he experiences it! Is he mute? It's certainly possible. How little does he understand? While his parents, one a counterfeit, communicate to each other solely in a form and syntax unintelligible to all but the person speaking it – in the densest poetry of a private language…

But I'm getting carried away. Three beers in the sun and I'm anyone's – so what happens when I'm already engaged before I even enter a bar for the first? Is this why I came to Spain? To splurge my great-uncle's bequest to me – my avuncular death-dividend – on a white brick shack in the harsh white sun in the blasted hills of Andalucía, with an acre of earth and stubborn goats and a stubborn wife whose idiom, evolving with the years, resists my every attempt at analysis, and whose son refuses to speak at all and perhaps understands even less than that – her lucky Jim who is, I suspect, allergic – yes, in a sensory sense – allergic to formal irregularity…

Is this why I came to Spain? – *really?*

Well, it sounds okay so far…

I think my wife may be drunk as well. At any rate, she's flushed.

"What is your name?" she is asking me. "I don't even know what is your name!" Her father watches us without expression, his forearms on the bar.

"Dave," I say, which isn't true.

A PLAGUE OF WOMEN

Every year in the hot months our town is afflicted by a plague of women. Nobody knows where they come from or where they go the rest of the year. Nobody knows when the plague first occurred or why, but the oldest residents of the town claim to remember a time before the visitations began, when the worst one had to contend with in the hot months was cockroaches, spoilt milk, and the occasional dead dog in the street that nobody wanted to be responsible for burying. But now such concerns appear trivial, even ridiculous by comparison. How funny it seems!

The women range in height dramatically from about eight centimetres to just over a metre in height, with roughly an equivalent arm-span, and as a result they are able to access all sorts of nooks and crannies, they encroach and accumulate everywhere, and no one method of elimination is effective against them. Of course the residents take concerted action to resist their spread, the spring months are spent in interminable negotiations as to what the new year's measures will be, what they will cost and who will pay, but no matter the eventually agreed-upon strategy or the specifics of its implementation, every year it is very quickly everyone for themselves. Inevitably, we each hope only to protect our own homes from infestation, knowing full well that it is futile – the women get in everywhere. They swarm and squabble in behind bins, they cling to shower curtains, get trapped in sinks, or they fly out of cupboards, naked and shrieking. I myself know of a resident who found one in his breakfast cereal, and she laughed at him as he tried in vain to smash her with a frying pan, succeeding only in breaking the table.

EYE TEST

The letter came telling me that I was due my eye test. I went along the following week, almost without thinking about it, having met a friend for coffee and found myself in the area. I had not made the decision to go for my eye test – I had no appointment – but since I was there on the same street, having walked that way after saying goodbye to my friend, I went in.

I showed the man in the shop my letter. He was wearing a red tie. He told me the price, which was more than I could ever have imagined but also, strangely, in line with what I had expected. There was not to be any negotiation. In fact this kind of haggling is just not what anyone does any more, almost as if it was criminal to try and pay less than the price requested. Unless, that is, you are buying a house, in which case the rules are completely different, and it's perfectly normal to ask to pay less by multiples of what you might earn in a year. The friend I had just seen, as it happened, had been telling me in detail about exactly this process, as he and his partner were buying a house, or rather trying to – for it was still not certain, after many months, whether their progress up until that point would in due course culminate in the house becoming theirs. No doubt this was the reason that I started thinking about house-buying in the context of the otherwise frowned-upon art of haggling. Although "art" is perhaps a generous word. From what I had been told by my friend, it was normal for a prospective buyer to put in an offer that was lower than the asking price by two or three times their annual salary, whatever that might be, only for the seller, unperturbed, to reject this offer but make a counter-offer of, say, nine months' salary lower than the original amount. All this might take place within a matter of minutes, and without the buyer and the seller even speaking to one another, both offer and counter-offer instead being relayed by the estate agent over the phone. At which point the haggling may begin in earnest. Or rather, not perhaps quite in earnest, as both buyer and seller may well mistrust the estate agent and, never having spoken let alone met in person, likewise resent and mistrust one another. Nevertheless, the opportunity for a sale to be made can be gauged very quickly by the estate agent, who is not himself (for they are almost always "hims") having to reach an agreement by adding or subtracting such eye-watering sums of their own theoretical earnings – and so are the chief beneficiaries of a "neutrality" the terms of which neither buyer nor seller much appreciate (which is to say, a "neutrality" in which they only halfway believe). This means, in the best case scenario, that the estate agent is able to reassure both parties that the other isn't really serious about the price being asked or offered and a compromise figure can therefore be reached – a figure which the estate agent seems to have had in mind as "a serious offer" from the start, and will often have taken the helpful step of suggesting it to the buyer before he designates it as such on relaying it to the seller...

Anyway I was thinking about this as I sat in the chair by the window of the eye test shop (the main function of which is, of course, to sell people spectacles, with or without a preliminary eye test) and watched the passers-by in the street, having booked an appointment only twenty-five minutes later. I was thinking about house-buying and home-owners and "the property ladder" and how strange it was that any of this could come to be considered normal, or indeed as a rite of passage or initiation into adulthood, while in other less "civilized" parts of the world one might, at an earlier age, have to kill something with a spear and eat it. Perhaps somewhere in the Amazon rainforest an elder was explaining to the young of the tribe the strange rituals of city-dwellers and their various different types of mortgage.

Whether I was waiting for twenty-five minutes or less or more I'm not sure, but either way it wasn't long before the man in the red tie ushered me into a separate room in which my eye test was to be undertaken – or *conducted* might be the better term, as it's not the same as other tests in that you can't in any meaningful way prepare. The man in the red tie didn't say anything and, having opened the door, somewhat abruptly closed it behind me. In the same moment, also without speaking, the eye test lady gestured for me to sit in the black leather chair attached to the floor on the far side of the room in conjunction with the surprisingly un-state-of-the-art-looking eye test machinery. She was a brunette of average height and pretty rather than beautiful, in grey skirt, black tights and simple black shoes – and for some reason I couldn't pin down, together with the eye test machinery, she reminded me of the James Bond movies I watched on video at my friend's house as a child. But I did not have long to consider this impression since the eye test lady turned off the lights the instant that I was sitting down in the black leather chair.

She then instructed me, via a guiding hand on the back of my head, to put my eyes to the binocular-type element set at the corresponding height of the eye test machinery, through which I could see the capital letters in descending rows, each row made up of smaller capitals than the letters of the row above. Meanwhile the eye test lady adjusted the dials on the eye test machinery to bring the letters in and out of focus.

"Okay," she said. "Tell me what you see."

"Letters," I said. "Capitals. Big ones to start with and then –"

"Yes," said the eye test lady, "I already know that. What I mean is: read them out."

I started to read the letters out but she stopped me almost at once. "Hold on," she said, "I've done this wrong. You're supposed to close one eye and read them out then. First one eye and then the other. We could test both eyes together but it wouldn't really tell us much. Let's do your left eye first. Or the right one…"

I could see her legs, grey skirt, black tights, to the right of my own legs as I looked down – but the moment I moved my head a fraction away from the binocular element the eye test lady's hand was there as a block and prompt to return my eyes to the warm plastic rims and the capital letters.

"Just close one eye and let's try again…"

My right eye open, my left eye closed, I began to read the letters from the top row down, leaving a gap of a second or two between each letter for no reason other than because this seemed appropriate in test conditions, not because I needed the time to move my eyes from one letter to the next, or to recognize them.

Therefore I proceeded slowly. The capital letters were still easily legible four rows down, then five rows down, over thirty seconds later. I felt confident that I could spend a minute or even ninety seconds reading the letters at this pace before experiencing any difficulty, and I was in no hurry to reach this threshold.

But the eye test lady interrupted. "Actually," she said, "this is boring." She removed her hand from the back of my head.

"Shall I switch to the other eye?"

"Well," said the eye test lady, "you can if you want to, but I expect it will be much the same. Unless you're really quite blind in that eye? But if you were, I expect you'd have noticed. Do you think you might be quite blind in that eye?"

"No," I said, "I don't think so."

My eyes were against the binocular element but I had enough space, with both eyes open, to look down at her legs, at her grey skirt, black tights and simple black shoes, which were angled so as to be pointing towards one another – by which I mean pointing at the imaginary point where their trajectories would eventually meet, by my estimation a few metres behind me out beyond the wall. Again I tried to move my eyes away from the eye test machinery but was prevented by her hand on the back of my head, firm but gentle like a primary school teacher.

"I know," said the eye test lady, "why don't we talk about something else?"

"Okay," I said. "Shall I still read the letters?"

"Read them, but don't read them out loud. Just tell me when you're having trouble seeing them and how many rows down that is, and that should tell us how blind you are. I mean, not that you're necessarily blind, I'm sure you'd have noticed if you were, but you know... where they get too small."

"First one eye and then the other?"

"Or both at once," she said. "It doesn't really matter."

It was okay with me. By this point, of course, I was sexually and romantically fascinated by the eye test lady, whom on first sight I had evaluated as merely conventionally pretty, not beautiful, and whose face I hadn't seen again since beginning the eye test procedure. But this was neither here nor there. The last time I had visited the doctor's surgery I became similarly fixated on the young American locum doctor who asked me questions about how often I needed the toilet and whether it hurt to urinate in response to my report of a minor complaint which had resolved itself soon afterwards without diagnosis. She had also asked me if I was a smoker and I said that I was when I wasn't.

"Now," said the eye test lady, "I can tell that you're aroused. I suppose you're imagining me taking my clothes off, or pushing your face between my legs, or bending me over something and ripping my tights off – something along those lines?"

"Yes," I said, "along those lines."

"Because I'm standing near you and wearing tights?"

"I suppose so," I said. "Because you're standing near me."

"The tights are so to speak circumstantial? Keep reading the letters, please."

"I am," I said, "I'm on the seventh row."

"Very good. So it's not that I'm particularly attractive, or the skirt, or the tights, it's just that I'm standing near you and I'm a woman. Would you say that's accurate?"

"Yes," I said. "More or less."

"You're imagining me taking my clothes of?"

"Not specifically. But I suppose so, yes."

"But you realise that's not going to happen?"

"Yes. But I can't stop thinking about it."

"I'm sure it's not helpful, now that I've said it. Before it was just a vague idea, but now I've made it *specific* for you. Now you're specifically imagining it, ripping my tights off, or whatever."

"Rolling down your tights," I said. "Your feet pushing off your shoes."

"I see," said the eye test lady. "Can you still read the letters?"

"I don't know, I keep going back to the beginning. I think I get to the ones I can't read and I get distracted and have to go back. It's hard to concentrate."

"Hmm," said the eye test lady. "You must try harder. Hard. Harder. How about that?"

"Tights and ripping them off and fucking."

"Keep reading the letters, please."

"I am. I am. They're getting blurry."

"All men are rapists," said the eye test lady. "Masturbation turns you blind. The world could be organized in such a way so that everyone had enough to eat – so why isn't it? Is it because we don't care? And what about global warming? Isn't global warming scary? If you want to you can imagine that I let you put your hand on my thigh. Up my skirt and on my thigh. You understand that it's not going to happen, but I don't mind if you imagine it."

"I can't see anything. I'm going blind."

"It's perfectly normal," said the eye test lady. "You were blind to begin with, and in the end you'll go blind again. Imagine your hand against my thigh. You're a man. It's not your fault."

It sounded like the eye test lady was at least slightly breathy, slightly excited, but the blood in my head and my loss of vision, as well as my general condition, made it impossible to know with any certainty. Her inside leg, lower down, not her thigh, was pressed against the outside of my knee, while my eyes were pressing harder and harder against the warm plastic rims of the binocular element of the eye test machinery, and her hand gripped my hair. The whole world was rushing and whirling around me. Her inside knee against my outside knee. I was blind. There was no way back.

Afterwards she apologised for calling me a rapist.

"That's okay," I said.

"Have you got a family?"

"Yes," I said.

"Kids?"

"A daughter."

"Mother?"

"Yes."

"They wouldn't like me calling you a rapist."

"No," I agreed.

"A bit rapey, maybe. But not a rapist."

There wasn't much else to say.

I wondered if the man in the red tie next door was in some way the pimp of the eye test lady. But it didn't seem likely. Surely it was too complicated to set up a spectacles shop as a front, to send out the letters and so on and so forth, relying on the eye test lady's hypothesis that all men were "a bit rapey" in order to identify and consolidate the customer base? After all, I had been willing to pay a surprising sum of money – without haggling – simply in order to receive an eye test, without any expectation of a sexual encounter. Although perhaps, given how readily I had consented to being so to speak exploited, to try and claim I had *no expectation* of a sexual encounter wasn't tenable. I had not been *expectant* of a sexual encounter, but the possibility of a sexual encounter had presented itself to me without delay as soon as I had entered the room – it had presented itself to me *at the drop of a hat*, was the best way I could think to describe it.

"Anyway, I think your eyes are fine," said the eye test lady. "And you're not a rapist."

"Thanks," I said. "That's good to know."

"And you don't have to look through there any more."

"Through where?" I said. "Oh yeah…"

When I moved my head from the eye test machinery, the eye test lady was sitting on a chair by the window to the room next door. The man in the red tie was talking to another customer by the spectacle display stand by the entrance. She was sort of slouched down in her chair like she was pretending to be a teenager, bored by the class she was in at school. She was also watching the man in the red tie, or else looking past him out of the window at the passers-by in the street.

THE RULES

Like any place really, there were some things you were allowed to do and some things you weren't. The list was projected onto the wall. The things that you weren't allowed to do was in bright red, the rest of it in navy blue. Everything was in capitals, so you knew. That way no one could complain if they broke one of the rules and were summoned to the top man's office to face the consequences. And no one did complain, either – since complaining was right at the top of the list of things that you weren't allowed to do.

But it wasn't easy. The rules, because they were comprehensive, were impossible to remember in their entirety, and they were also being constantly revised and updated. Plus the way that they were projected was not ideal. New projectors had been installed but – even if we weren't allowed to say it – the quality of the projection was actually worse than it had been with the old projectors, more blurry and shaky, while the whirring and clicking was now so loud you could hardly hear yourself think. It was so loud you sometimes started to wonder if what you were listening to was the sound of your brain on the way towards some form of collapse.

Not that it really mattered. All of us, when the lights were on, were required to be assembled along the length of the wall onto which the rules were being projected, which meant that we were always unavoidably in the way.

Every so often, by accident, somebody would break one of the rules and be summoned to the top man's office and pounded into a bloody mess by the top man's service administrator, while the rest of us watched through the glass.

SOME MEN

Some men are murderers. Some men wear a suit and tie and shave every morning and they eat their food with a knife and fork but they are murderers. Some men are rapists of women and torturers and rapists of other men and sometimes women but not so often the torturers of women, just the rapists, or if they are in a sexual and/or family relationship with them then they beat them up as well as rape them. Some men will tell you one thing but when you are not there to see it they do the other thing that they said that they wouldn't: they drink and fight or just beat up other men up who don't fight, or they take drugs, good ones and bad ones, and they gamble all their money away and fuck other women or just rape and/or beat them up and/or kill them and say they didn't. Some men have power but they feel insecure and only use their power to get more power by taking it away from other people who have less power, and they know that they're doing it but they say that they're not and/or they don't know that they're doing it but they do it twice as much if you tell them and/or they beat you up and kill you, especially if you're women. Some men send armies of other men to stop other men who they say are doing bad things, and they stop them by killing them and raping their women. Some men are lazy but most men work hard the whole time doing all the bad things they shouldn't. Some men urinate on the floor and don't clean it up. Some men are holy and only rape children.

But I'm not like that.

BEST MAN'S SPEECH

Good afternoon everybody.

I have been asked to say a few words about Michael on the occasion of this, his wedding to Lara. I don't know Michael well but I have been asked to do this because there is no one who knows him better. As you know, a best man's speech is supposed to contain some embarrassing comedic material about the groom, but ultimately paint a picture of him as a wonderful man and now husband. I'm afraid that this is not going to be possible in Michael's case as there is simply nothing funny to be said about him and much to say that Lara has chosen badly. I have known Michael for almost ten years, entirely by accident and without any effort or encouragement on my part or indeed on his – instead we have been placed together by the universe for reasons that are probably so to speak aesthetic, by which I mean that some banal formal logic might insist upon our proximity for want of a better solution. This is not intended as a religious statement. We are both undoubtedly failed human beings.

Lara, my speech will be making you uncomfortable, but I am trying to speak honestly. Why are you marrying Michael? There is no good reason to do this and you must know that you are jeopardizing the rest of your life. I can only assume that you somehow believe that by marrying Michael you can redeem him and in this magical altruistic act give purpose to your own existence. Lara, if this is the case, I urge you to consider in specific terms exactly how this is going to happen, and recognize that it's impossible. Your life is not a fairy tale. Michael is not a handsome prince.

Lara – save yourself!

RAYMOND

These days I have a car of my own. I sit in the back and my driver, Raymond, gets me where I need to go. To have my own driver is not essential to the way in which I make my living, which is based on a particular approach to the interactions of human beings. You could call it *my attitude to business*, although strictly speaking I am not a businessman. I do not own a business.

Nonetheless I am attached to Raymond, as I associate him with the good things in life. I associate him with my success.

Of course, before I became successful, I had nobody to drive me who would not expect me, at the very minimum, to talk to them as the price of their services – and this type of transaction, in which the terms have not been made explicit, is one I have never been able to tolerate. I would therefore have to use public transport. I would even, despite my deep misgivings, regularly have to travel by coach, because I was seeing a girl from Nottingham and the cheapest way to get there was by coach. I was young, and I didn't have any money. But I knew this was no excuse.

I didn't even like the girl – our relationship was transactional in precisely the way I had begun to resent – and the journey took at least four hours or longer if there was an accident.

So I would sit on this coach on the motorway, thinking: "I hate coaches. And here I am on a coach. I hate this girl. And here I am going to visit her – in Nottingham. On a coach…"

It was the middle of summer, sweltering, four or more hours travel ahead of me, and after that a whole weekend of this girl asking me: "What's the matter, honey? Anything you want to talk about?" When the whole time it was the talking that was bothering me in the first place. The talking as *a constant transaction*…

People would even sometimes try to talk to me on the coach too, as if I wasn't angry enough about the situation already.

"So why are you off to Nottingham, then?"

"Because I'm a fucking idiot. You?"

But the man that I punched hadn't tried to talk to me. He hadn't really done anything. Except that, every five minutes or so, he would snort or grunt to clear his throat.

He was just across the aisle from me and I could see at once that he was pathetic. He had greasy hair all pointing in slightly the wrong direction, thick-lensed glasses, a face somehow too fat for his features, and huge teeth that poked out of his mouth at almost a right angle to his head.

I was hot. Every other seat was taken.

Soon this man and his noises were the only thing I could think about. His greasy hair and hideous teeth and how long it would be until he next snorted or grunted as if his whole skull was full of phlegm and he was never going to do anything about it.

It was like he was pushing it in my face, saying: "Look! – look how pathetic I am! – I'm pathetic and I'm not going to let you forget it…" He could have bought shampoo, a comb and glasses that weren't an inch and a half thick. He could have paid for dental treatment. But instead he was just snorting and grunting more and more often and louder and louder. He knew that he was pathetic and he was using it as a provocation.

Thinking this, I got so angry that I started to worry about my health. "This man is so pathetic, he might actually kill me…"

And I thought: "I could punch him in the face."

Squirming down, wiping the blood with his sleeve, he suddenly looked about half the size he had the moment before. His skin had turned a clammy white and terror was in his eyes.

I wondered what was going to happen.

When a voice said: "Someone had to do it…"

Raymond is not a talkative man. After all these years I know nothing about him, and I don't have to think about what he's thinking because he never lets it show.

AT THE WEEKEND

The party was in this house outside town. We caught a bus to the nearest village and walked from there. There weren't any street-lights and we had to go up a gravel path under sycamore trees. There were two concrete lions by the front door and we could hear the noise of people inside and also around the back. Then a tall man in drag and a copper wig pulled open the door and told us that it wasn't his house. "But do come in!" he said, bowing and draping an arm. "Welcome! Welcome!"

Nobody knew whose house it was but there must have been two hundred people there, half of them in fancy dress, occupying every room and the garden as well. There was a garage with two sofas in it and a tennis court with the floodlights on. There was alcohol everywhere and drugs – pills and powders being shared around. People were lying about on the floor or dancing on the furniture. There were people in a walk-in cupboard playing Monopoly, only the light switch was outside the door so they kept shouting "Hey!" whenever someone turned it off. The biggest room had a piano in it. This tiny girl was lying on it and pretending that she was being seductive while a guy who was dressed up as Alice Cooper was hammering away at the keys and crooning – until she rolled off it onto the floor and then everyone was shrieking with laughter.

It started getting light. There were people outside still playing tennis and wherever we went there were more and more drugs being crushed up and chopped into lines and snorted. The house belonged to a guy called Mikey but no one knew who Mikey was. He was probably having sex in a bedroom. "To Mikey!" we all kept raising our glasses – and a different man on the piano improvised a ballad that was called *To Mikey*. There were people snogging. We all sang along.

Later I played a game of tennis with a German who said he was training to be an architect. He was older than me but he still hadn't qualified. "Forever," he said. "It will take me forever! Come on, let's play tennis – serve me the ball!" I served and somehow it went over the net and somehow he managed to hit it back again. "To Mikey!" we screamed.

A DJ had desks set up in the garage. It was sunny outside but dark in the garage. Everyone was going nuts, and these white-shirted waiters were bringing round bowls of melon and mango and pineapple – unless they were just in fancy dress – and shaking up bottles of champagne and spraying them all over us.

There was no sign of anyone going home.

We felt like we could go on forever.

SANDWICHES AND DECKCHAIRS

"Look," said the man to those of us waiting, "I sympathise but it's not up to me, it's really not me who makes the decisions. Of course, if you wish to make a complaint, I understand completely, and I'm here to help however I can – the Complaints Procedure is why we're here. But what with there being so many of you, the whole process may take some time. I would also like to apologise to those new arrivals who have not been able to find a seat. My colleagues and I are doing our best to rectify this situation but please, if you could in the meantime stand in a calm and orderly fashion, that'd be wonderful. Your patience is appreciated."

He smiled and sighed, glanced at his watch, stood up and left through the door behind him. The door led to a flight of stairs with daylight somewhere at the top of them. The man would always leave it open. We waited behind the glass.

"Cup of tea," the man explained, reappearing down the stairs. "Have there been any refreshments yet? Hot drinks? Beverages? At least some plastic cups for the water cooler – or is the water cooler still…? I see…

"Well, I'm afraid that I can only apologise and again say how disappointed I am. I spoke to the Catering Manager *personally*, and he told me... Well, I can't say he *promised*, but I certainly felt that he *understood*... A cold buffet seems reasonable. Sandwiches, if that's what's available. But the Catering Manager, I have to admit, he hasn't been in the best of spirits since they told him... And of course I do understand his situation. What he's going through... For years now they've been shaving bits off – out-sourcing, restructuring, efficiency savings, whatever they're calling it – *a resourcing issue*, that's the latest – and it's got to the point where you can't pretend that the organization, if I'm being honest...

"I mean look, nostalgia or not, we can all agree that it's not how it used to be, when you really felt that your colleagues, from whichever part of the organization, were all pulling in the same direction, that they *shared the values*...

"But I don't know... Maybe it *is* just nostalgia..."

And closing his eyes he began to sing: "*See the girl standing over there? She used to be mine, but not any more – can you see the girl standing over there? Watch – she's walking out that door...*"

Opening his eyes again, the man looked embarrassed and he coughed, shaking this feeling from him.

"Of course," he said, "some of the things that have changed have changed for the better, I can't deny it – so take off your rose-tinted spectacles, as the Catering Manager likes to say, there's no use getting dewy-eyed about things you can't do nothing about. Facts are facts and that's all there is to it... Where before there was a team of sixteen and that was just here in Complaints, now there's only the five of us and we're supposed to be covering Admin too...

"But Catering – okay, their remit changed – but Catering is down to three and *as you can see* it's not enough. That's the *fact*..."

He hesitated. "Not that I'm saying you're wrong to complain

55

– I'm not. That may be the party line but I for one am not going to tow it… I can see that you're here… *in good faith* – I mean you only have to open your eyes… But the fact is," he shook his head, shrugged and sighed, "there *are* just so many more of you than there ever were before…

"So I try and reason with him, of course I do. I tell him what I've been telling him since the last restructure twelve months ago. These people, I say, they still need to eat – sister franchise, sub-contracted or voluntary partner, it doesn't matter. Food is a basic requirement. Human beings are human beings. They're waiting to start the Complaints Procedure and they could be waiting days, weeks, longer – nobody seems to know. And in the meantime, every day, there's more arriving. More and more. Don't ask me why or where they come from – because I don't know. But in this job, I try and tell him, you have to try and have *empathy* – because that's what this job teaches you. It teaches you…"

He looked away.

"In any case, the Catering Manager, I know that he knows all this – I should think he knows it better than anyone! So I'd hoped if there couldn't be sandwiches that there might at least be some light refreshments… And – whatever *the current climate* – I'd hoped at least that the water cooler…"

He was sad – but he knew he could not be sad.

"Now those chairs, on the other hand, we might just be able to do something about…"

The man returned, empty-handed.

"I'm sorry," he said, "but nobody for the life of them can re-member where they're stashed away. The deckchairs. There's a roof, you see?" he pointed at the stairs through the door behind him, "and during the summer my colleagues and I enjoy a cup of tea up there. There isn't a railing so we sit well back – but the skyline…" There was delight in his eyes. "But anyway, what with the weather now, the seasons – I suppose it's been a while… I was convinced they were in the cupboard along with the rest of the summer gear, and I'm sure that this was *since* the restructure, so unless someone's been moving them… Not that there'd have been enough for all of you in any case – you'd have had to take turns, or nominate people. Draw straws." He started to laugh. "Surely, if I argued my case – if I took it to the highest people – surely we could get some straws…"

Often there were long periods in between the man leaving and returning again, but this was time was longer than before. We waited, standing shoulder to shoulder, watching the light that fell on the stairs beyond the door behind the glass.

Finally we saw his feet.

The tears were brimming around his eyes and fell each time he closed them. It was in some way our most hopeful moment.

He spoke in a voice that shook with fury.

"Despite what some of you may have heard, Michael Stokes, the Catering Manager, was a good man. He was dedicated. He cared about the people who worked in his kitchen. He cared about his customers. Michael Stokes… *cared about food*. He was, if not of *the very top grade*, then undoubtedly *a good chef*, well above average and… *committed to improving*. He never complained about making food for so many staff, week in, week out, in circumstances that anyone could see were unsatisfactory – the *resourcing issue* as they insist we call it… There was only so much a man could do…

"But Michael Stokes made a fantastic lasagne. He still – even at the end – he made a fantastic lasagne – and his chicken masala – his chicken masala…" He wiped his snot and his tears away.

A new hardness entered his voice.

"He never complained about making lunch for an organization that every year was diversifying, with new directorates, executives, specialists – the men and women drafted in to see the bigger picture and to make *the necessary changes*… But Michael Stokes would not complain. He wouldn't, he wasn't that kind of person…

"I asked him… for *sandwiches*…

"I know that other people asked…

"But Michael Stokes… Michael Stokes…" he wiped his snot and clenched his fist, "Michael Stokes was a good man – a man of truth, of principle. He saw things clearly, Michael Stokes. He understood the way of the world. But he wanted to cook – that was all. He wanted to work for the organization that he'd always worked for – *in-house*. He didn't care about marketing and he wasn't… he wasn't *a numbers man*… But what does any of it mean any more, if a man like that… a *human being*…

"We needed railings!" he banged the desk. "Everyone said it: we needed railings. But the organization, did anyone listen when everyone we needed railings…?"

His sadness had turned to a fragile anger we could see that he wasn't comfortable with. He looked at each of us who were waiting and he shook his head, determined.

"But I won't blame you! Whatever anyone else is saying, I will not place the blame on people – also human beings – who have come to us in good faith with the simple desire – the lawful and legitimate desire – to make a complaint, nothing more. To register their dissatisfaction with services rendered or received…"

The tears were flowing down his face and he spoke with an overload of feeling. "The Complaints Procedure…" he gasped and wept, "the Complaints Procedure is *why we're here*…"

The new man was younger with hate in his eyes. His voice, low but getting louder, crept out between his pale lips and took no notice of the glass: it was everywhere. We listened as if we were falling asleep: as if time were oxygen and finite.

"First of all," the man began, "I want to say that my predecessor has explained to me your situation. I appreciate that some of you have been waiting now for many days. Some of you, I understand, have been waiting for not only days and weeks but months and even, they tell me, years. They tell me that you are hungry, that some of you here have not found seats and that some of you, in transit or in events relating to your arrival, may have sustained injuries that require urgent medical attention. There are some of you, they also tell me, who are sick and require medicine or diseased and requiring antibiotics – and that you will need to be treated immediately at the risk of the contagion spreading.

"They tell me also," the man continued, "that the water cooler is broken, and that Maintenance, as of the first of the month, are no longer part of the service core. It cannot therefore be specified exactly when they will come to fix it, although we have the assurance of the Strategy Team that the matter has been prioritized and will be attended to as soon as possible. I apologise for this inconvenience – they have asked me to apologise.

"But as for myself," the man leant forward, "I can only say that those who have chosen to avail themselves of the Complaints

Procedure should not be attempting to place blame upon anyone *other than themselves*. Each of you has made their choice and this choice is what has led you here. To this basement. Lacking the most basic amenities. With no means to influence your situation or escape from your predicament…

"I know that there will be some amongst you that feel that justice has not been done. Some amongst you, I also know, will hate me for telling you this – *the truth*. I can feel that you are burning with a terrible rage – a rage you feel to be righteous on the basis of these injustices that you feel that you have suffered…

"But I welcome this hate with joy…

"I welcome this hate because I know what it is: the realisation of *responsibility*. For this is your reality – yours and *yours alone*… This hatred is what you've been hiding from in shame and fear from the very beginning – from a time which you no longer even remember – and it is nothing more than the realisation and the humiliation that follows from it. A realisation and a humiliation from which – from today – you will no longer hide…

"Do you finally understand?' The man was standing. "There will be no sandwiches! There will be no sandwiches or bandages or antibiotics! Tomorrow there will be more of you but the situation will remain the same. Those who sit or lie on the floor will be trampled upon by the new arrivals. Those of you who die will die and your bodies will not be taken away. Those of you who are close to dying will not be treated with preference…

"There will be no sandwiches!" the man screamed and banged his fist on the glass. "Do you finally understand? There will be no sandwiches!"

And watching him we felt our bodies swell with the confidence of children who run and jump and trip and fall and yet never remember to be afraid.

MAN WITH A PRAM

Expert and experienced man with a pram can procure babies of most descriptions at short notice for willing buyers in the UK and beyond. Discreet and reliable service promised with comprehensive official paperwork, birth certificates, details of legal adoption or overseas purchase, etc. All babies housed at your convenience for all-inclusive attachment recovery period at purpose-built wet nurse facility and delivered in perfect/original physical condition and quality gender-neutral clothing. Deluxe ethnic babies also available for special occasions/holiday rental. Prices exclude VAT and may be subject to indemnity charges.

OLD PEOPLE

Residents are hereby advised to refrain from leaving old people with other refuse for collection. Old people surplus to household requirements should be taken to the tip where a £50 processing fee will apply.

EGGSHELLS

The eggshells are a real problem. A year or so after we moved into the house, we began to notice them. Not every room was similarly affected. The back room (the "study") had only a dusting, the guest room was virtually untouched, and here in the utility room the concrete floor meant the eggshells were easy enough to sweep away. But in the hallways and communal areas and especially up the first flight of stairs (the guest room being at the top of the second) the accumulation of eggshells was a fact of our existence it was impossible to wish away. Of course we doubted our sanity. In the twilight of our unease, a throwaway joke could morph into the gravest of conspiracies and so form the basis of our interactions for the rest of the day or the week. An array of products and pesticides – gels, sprays, powders, mousses – colonised our cupboards and shelves and itself became central to our sense of encroachment. We felt like gameshow contestants, cringing at the half-baked irony of our every attempt to communicate, while a studio audience we couldn't see would roar and applaud each failed catchphrase. In time we almost ceased to speak except to clarify pointless details or argue uncontrollably about hypothetical rights and wrongs.

At night I stand in the utility room, a slow white moon in the window above me, considering the gap between the world as I imagined it and my cold bare feet in this sea of fragments.

We do not resemble the people we are.

HAMSTERS

I spend all my time walking and all my time thinking but I don't know where any of it leads. I assume I have responsibilities and so I am anxious about my failure to meet them, to do the things I am supposed to do, and I worry that I am walking away from my responsibilities, in fact that I am running away, but there's no way of knowing if this is the case, there are no clues, the landscape is made up of details all of which are incidental, my mind churns every feature into the same spongey, indigestible horsemeat, this mechanical churn is all I hear, and so I just carry on, or don't, I turn around, or left, right, I veer abruptly whenever possible, into parks, carparks, cemeteries, along alleyways, between lines of gardens, up and down runs of wide stone steps, and in every case I am all the more anxious about the choice that I have made, or been *compelled to make*, and unbearably aware of the absence of purpose to whatever path, or *absence of path*, I am presently wasting my time in pursuit of. I accept that I am not of sound mind but I don't know what this is supposed to achieve. I accept that I am *struggling.*

There are obstructions whichever route you take. The obstructions are a fact of so little concern to me that often I barely register that I am clambering over, or crawling under, or breaking a path through the middle of them. In fact I require obstructions to convince me that I am on the right track, nonsensical as this clearly is, whether natural or man-made, animal, vegetable, mineral, I confront and attack and feed on obstructions as if with the frenzy of lust, as if – *regardless of whether or not I notice* – to attack and overcome an obstruction might cause the whole auditorium to rise up and applaud this latest senseless climax to my solitary pantomime.

I remember once a wardrobe that was wedged six inches from the ground at the exit of a narrow alley I had entered from the other end, so that my only option was to smash my way through it using forehead, elbows, knees, shins – a frenzied yet laborious process – until, wet with sweat and bloodied, splinters in my face and gums, at last I broke on through…

A group of smokers was outside a pub and my entrance caused them great delight.

"Where have you come from?" a woman asked.

"From Narnia!" another shouted.

"From breakfast with my mother in Debenham's!" I screamed, shaking a fist at them. "From breakfast in Debenham's, you shits!" and I lurched myself into the crowd, which shrieked, as the men stepped forward to quieten me.

I may have been to Debenham's a hundred times for breakfast with my mother. Without any memory of having made the arrangement, over and again I find myself sitting opposite my mother in the café upstairs, at a table by the window with a view of the sea.

My mother has a pot of tea and a scone with a small bowl of jam for spooning, while I have the breakfast that comes first on the list, their standard edible obstruction, which I consume as if I have just been told the building has been set on fire. She is either my mother or my grandmother, a confusion that has endured.

This is roughly our conversation:

"How are you, William?" says my mother/grandmother.

I scrape and clash my cutlery and make sexual noises as I suck down the food.

"William? I know you can hear me. William, please tell me how you are."

"I'm okay. I'm doing really great, actually. I love my job, and I've met a wonderful woman, and we've settled down and started a family. We have two boys, Erik and Thor – because Giselle, their mother, is Norwegian – and they go to the local school, which is a really good school. In fact it's *outstanding*. They have a school play every Christmas which Giselle does the make-up for, and this year Erik got the leading role – he's playing Count Dracula! And Thor got A's in all his exams and he wants to be a lawyer. Or a web designer… And he's vegan. Did I tell you Thor is a vegan? The fussy little fucking shit! A vegan, we cook him separate meals!"

My mother/grandmother has put down her scone.

"It's true – you can look it all up online…"

"William!" my mother/grandmother whispers. "Erik and Thor were your hamsters when we lived in Denmark Hill with your father. Do you remember that, William? Please, I'm very worried about you. William, you haven't shaved…"

I think a lot about that wardrobe. It can't have just been left there by accident when they realised too late that it wouldn't fit through. Surely, if this were the case, they'd have carried it by its narrower ends? It must have been put there *deliberately to form an obstruction* – and so for me to smash my way through it.

I think about my father, too.

My father who would make me squat with my back against the wall, until the pain in my thighs won out. Stealing, he'd say. That was why. Except that I hadn't stolen anything, and so I could only interpret it as *lack of effort* he meant. I had not worked hard enough and had let him down. His wife/mother could do nothing to stop him punishing me as necessary.

Years on I saw him again. I went by train. The sun shone into the carriage and I had enough money to buy a sandwich. He was the youngest man in the home by far. All he wants to do is drink, they told me. They filled his glass from a bottle in his cupboard. He slept in a turquoise plastic armchair. On the drawers by the bed was a jar of raisins. The room was dark. Sometimes he'll eat a raisin, they told me. Not often. He's been sleeping today. Ring the bell if he wets himself. Nobody checked with anyone if I was who I said I was. They went to feed lunch to other people, some were outside in the garden. He was the oldest in the home by far. Only his hair was still alive, a strange, billowing head of hair, attached to his scalp like a tent in the wind. He didn't wake up. I stole the raisins.

"William… William…" my mother/grandmother is holding my hand. "William, you have to get help. You can't be alone like this all your life. You can't be so angry like this all your life. There must be somewhere you can go. There must be something… A drop-in centre?"

I weep onto my Heinz baked beans and streaky bacon and cumberland sausage. "I loved those hamsters," I grip her hand. "I loved those lazy fucking hamsters…"

"I know you did, William. And they loved you…"

ANONG

Twice a week I follow my wife around the Asian supermarket. I carry the basket and Anong walks two or three metres ahead, shouting the name of the product she's heading for so that people know to get out of the way. In fact I'm not completely sure what the purpose of the shouting is, whether it's for my benefit or for hers. The aisles are much less strictly arranged than they are in the supermarkets I used to go to: maybe she can't ever fully remember where the thing is that she's looking for, and she shouts it out to help her find it. It may be she's not even intending to say it out loud, or quite *that loud*. It's just what she does. They have different ways of doing things, Thai people. They're Buddhists, they have all the monks and the temples, but they're not like the Buddhists you get over here. They're not afraid of an argument.

I've been with Anong since I've had my new face.

———————

The accident happened in Thailand on the day before I was getting married, and I was getting married in exactly the way you imagine the moment you hear about a man getting married in Thailand – I'd seen her photo on my computer, and I was paying her to marry me. I hadn't told anyone what I was doing – I told my brother I was going to Brussels, to this day I have absolutely no idea why. I hired the moped from a lady by the airport on the island where I was meeting my wife and her family that afternoon. I would be staying the night in her village and the ceremony was the following morning.

But I didn't make it to her village. I flew my moped off the road on the way down the mountain to it, when a guy and his daughter in a pick-up truck came up on the left-hand side, his right, my left – and in Thailand they drive on the same side as us. Or at least they're supposed to. The last thing I saw before losing consciousness was their faces looking down at me over the edge of the roadside, watching, then disappearing.

I can't remember anything about the first days in hospital. I don't know if I was in a coma or just heavily sedated, and even once I was awake again they still couldn't give me a lot of detail. It was a small hospital on the island with about a hundred beds and there was only one doctor there who spoke any English, who'd seen enough tourists have moped accidents to not have much sympathy any more. To be fair, about twenty percent of the ward were Western men who'd had moped accidents, although none of them as bad as mine, so you could see where he was coming from. We were wasting his time. Then again, the whole place is basically set up for tourists to get into moped accidents. Usually they just break a limb or smash a few ribs or need some stitches. Not so many are so lucky to need extensive facial reconstructive surgery without being completely dead: the other kind of crash they have. I remember lying in the hospital and thinking about this – how lucky I was and how *unlucky* – going back and forth and back and forth between these points of view, watching the nurses on their round going back and forth as well.

Every so often, to break things up, I was visited by the ghost of my mother who died when my brother and I were kids, and who was understandably shocked and upset by the way that things had turned out in her absence. Especially by my moped accident and the whole internet marriage bit.

It was nice to see her. I think I knew that she wasn't real, but she wasn't completely unreal either – you don't get visited every week by the ghost of your mother, morphine or otherwise, so I knew she had some kind of substance to her.

"What could make you so unhappy that you'd do this?" she asked me. "I never worried about you, Joe. Was I wrong not to worry? I always thought you'd be okay…"

"I'm alright, mum," I said to her. "I was just lonely, that's all."

"You won't be lonely," said my mum. "You won't."

———————

The hospital where I had the surgery was a private one here in England, different in pretty much every way from the ward in Ko Chang, where I'd been kept in a very placid condition by the morphine and the occasional reminder "*No screaming!*" when they'd let the dosage drop. This time I had my own room, not a ward, with a red button to press for assistance. At first I didn't like to press it, but once I got to know the nurses I used to press it a lot more often, depending which of them were on. There was one nurse who was Thai herself and she was honestly the kindest and most lovely person I had ever met – I guess she was better paid than her compatriots back home – but she only came in the one time near the beginning to change my dressings, and I never saw her again. I remember I started talking to her about the feeling of sailing over the precipice, my hands gripped tight to the handlebars but the rest of me sprawling, unattached, a sparkling sea on the horizon – the whole sensation had stayed with me, as if it was somehow still playing out and the part where I smashed into the tree and tumbled down through the branches wasn't the only possible outcome. And the Thai nurse said she was from the North, from Chiang Mai, and had never been to the islands. "But Ko Chang is very beautiful," she told me, smiling.

I was waiting for the next time I saw her to ask her what the North was like, and how she found it living in England, but for whatever reason she never came back. Maybe she moved to a different ward, or even a different hospital, or maybe it was just a coincidence that I wasn't ever her patient again. Or maybe she wasn't real either. In any case, I wasn't going to get too hung up on a girl I had only met once – and who might have been a hallucination – when there were so many other nurses about tending to me on a daily basis, who were often quite lovely as well. In fact I ended up proposing to several nurses over the months I was there and got myself a bit of a reputation.

It was a funny time. Of course I didn't have much of a face, or at least not one you'd want to marry, but in some sort of way there was a freedom in that and it gave me a sort of courage. Meanwhile, on the nurses' side, there was always the possibility that the surgeons would excel themselves and the man in the bandages would turn out to be a bit of a catch once they'd finished. They used to joke with me about it. Instead of Joe they started calling me Mel, from that film *The Man Without A Face*, and that led on to them calling me Braveheart. After a while I used to put on a

Scottish accent when I was proposing marriage. I reckon a couple half-considered it, but you could tell there'd been a meeting and the official answer was no. I guess it makes sense that it's frowned upon. There's probably a lot of red tape involved.

The strange thing was, until the crash, I'd not had much confidence in myself with women. I know it wasn't just the drugs. As I said, it was like I was suddenly free. There was nothing left to be afraid of – except the loneliness, which my mum had banned.

That was why, the more I thought about it, the more it felt like flying to Thailand to marry a stranger was the bravest thing I ever did. I couldn't properly remember how I'd come to make the decision. It happened fast. I went along to this festival in a park that was a Thai festival. It was mainly just food stalls, beads and every size of decorative elephant, plus a stage with a lady in a green and gold sequined dress haranguing the crowd to keep dancing. But obviously most of the people there were Thai women and their husbands and kids. White husbands, mixed kids, and whole groups of friends and families out together for the day. I hadn't been expecting it. I went home and went on the internet and the next month I was flying out there. I'd never been to Thailand, or South-East Asia. I'd not even been on a moped before.

It was after a few weeks back in England that it dawned on me I'd already paid for half my new wife before the accident. Unfortunately I didn't have any money left due to the excess on my insurance, plus the fact that I'd now been off work for two months (which the Trade and Retail were very understanding about: they sent me a card and everything). Also, between the various stages of surgery my head was entirely wrapped in bandages, so I couldn't be sure if the image I had of my nearly-wife from another life was anything like the reality. But I didn't care much about any of that. The fact was, I needed her.

The disorientation that comes with a spell in this condition – the nurses called it "bandage-blind" – is a frightening thing for a person to go through. Some of the dreams and visions I had made the visits of my dead mum in Thailand seem perfectly reasonable.

There was one hallucination involving Gary Lineker hosting Match Of The Day. He was asking Alan Shearer about what he thought was wrong with me, which Shearer was saying was just about everything, and the two of them were dissecting me in a completely literal sense of the word. I couldn't see what they were up to exactly but they were getting right down to the nitty-gritty. Diagrams of mind and matter, with blunt diagnoses of all my shortcomings – spectacles, testicles, wallet and watch. It was horrific. Their designer shirts were drenched in blood and the disappointments they found in my entrails were being explained to everyone. Gary Lineker kept asking if there were any positives to be taken at all, and Alan Shearer kept solemnly saying: "No Gary, not that I can see. None whatsoever."

———————

Anong is actually the cousin of the woman I was on my way to marry. As I'd paid only half the price for Kuanjai, it was explained to me by her mother that she would not be proceeding with the marriage. I suppose by agreeing the higher price to begin with, before I had the accident and needed a replacement face, I hadn't created favourable conditions from which to negotiate. But since I *had* paid half and there was apparently no possibility of this money being reimbursed, Anong was to be my wife instead. She would be boarding a flight to England the following week. I went to the airport to meet her.

Anong doesn't like Kuanjai very much and assures me that I was fortunate to marry her and not her cousin. She tells me Kuanjai was by no means a virgin when we were engaged, having slept with so many Western men she could have been a ladyboy. She says Kuanjai would never have been happy with the small house and the "so-so" standard of living that I am able to provide, and that Kuanjai is very lazy and would refuse to go shopping and cook the dinner. She also says, due to all the make-up she wears, that Kuanjai has terrible skin. But she knows I don't care about any of this. I never even met Kuanjai. All I saw was a photo and I made a decision – not to be lonely. That's the only thing that matters.

"But Anong," I point at the surgeon's work when she tells me just how lucky I am, "I haven't got any skin at all…"

"Ha ha funny Joe, so what?" she says. "Plastic easy to clean."

MUNTERS

Everybody has seen the munters and yet many questions remain. What – please – has happened to them? Did the munters choose to be munters? Or was being munters chosen for them? Do they stay munters forever? Or is it a condition they grow out of? It seems to depend. Most of the munters are young, but they grow old quickly. Some appear to have been old for a very long time. They look like they were born that way, ravaged and twitchy, as if they know nothing new is left and accept this with a crafty wisdom, while the younger munters blink and gape like baby monkeys in the sun. They are compelling. I watch them in the mornings when they come to my shop to buy milk and vodka and fruit juice and cigarettes and always one of them will buy a pasty and the other munters will treat this as crazy but then immediately change their mind – they want a pasty after all – and they also want eighteen cans of beer. Their clothes are dirty and they smell, they stumble about and can hardly stay upright, the whole thing takes a very long time as they can't remember why they are there, they get distracted, burst out laughing, leave the shop and come back again – another one wants to buy a pasty! – and they treat all money as communal and seem not to know who is going to pay until they reach the till. Then one of them pays for everything, volunteering at random. They wear strange hats and sunglasses and other kinds of fancy dress, and although their speech is garbled they are always very friendly.

My other customers do not like them.

NUMBERS

Now everyone had a number in the middle of their face in the place where their nose and mouth used to be. The numbers were sort of like skin but plastic. They were sort of skin-colours but you could tell the difference, and if you looked closely you could see where the numbers – which were almost always single digits – had been grafted onto people's faces. It looked like it had been done in a hurry with some hot and clanking machine.

No one was really clear how this new system was supposed to work so the government sent out a brochure which was also full of numbers, with photos of people with numbers in the middle of their faces going about their usual daily business – catching a bus, or walking around a lake in the park.

There was a photo of a family having a barbecue, even though they wouldn't be able to eat anything because their mouths had been replaced by numbers, and they wouldn't be able to smell the food and they couldn't talk to each other. It looked like they had been told to look happy but when you looked closer you could see they were scared. A sort of panic was in their eyes and all their sausages and chicken was burnt.

Outside town was a mega-warehouse full of all the old mouths and noses, crawling in rats and insects eating the flesh away from teeth and bone, and for the people who had to work there it was good that they couldn't taste or smell it. They just wished they couldn't hear it either.

LENNY

I stare at this man who sits before me, in Lenny's chair, talking
at me, his head bulging, expanding as he emits his words like the
universe is said to expand, simply with the passage of time, or
not simply, perhaps it's complicated, as the evolution of life on
the planet cannot in truth be said to be simple just because it's
what happened, or at least what *has* happened, up to now, first
bang, then bloom, a heating up, a cooling off, tectonic rupture
and displacement, oceans, mountains, fossil fuels, a slow bacterial
metamorphosis, from sludge to slime to snake to snail to insect, six
legs, four legs, mammals, bipeds, the sex trade, slavery, the spin-
ning jenny, sliced bread, and all the way on and up towards this
simpleton who now sits before me, in Lenny's chair, and tells me
that he is my supervisor, my *new* supervisor, not Lenny, and that
since this is our first supervision I must pay attention to what he's
saying, to the words emitted, their ebb and flop, and demonstrate
to him that I have understood and am ready to amend my practice
in direct accordance with the new procedures recently devised by,
and to be implemented at the instruction of, senior personnel in
the strategy team, or rather at the instruction of their minions,
assuming there to be several, or minion, if in fact there is only
one, this man sat before me, in Lenny's chair, his head bulging,

who is not Lenny.

"If you find yourself in an unsafe or emergency situation," he says, "do *not* press the button for assistance. Do you understand?"

"Where's Lenny?" I ask him.

"I'm afraid I'm not here to discuss that with you."

"Okay," I tell the man. "Understood."

DES AND LEN

Des and Len were firm friends. They had been friends forever, so the fact that Des was a crocodile whereas Len was a (very short) human being had never been an issue. They did everything together. Or at least they tried to. But for some reason recently this had become increasingly difficult as despite the closeness of their friendship (which both still declared to be the case) they often wanted to do different things.

For example, Len would say: "Why don't we go to the cinema? There's that new film – I mean not new, but it's the origin story to that other film, the old one. Which everyone says is a classic." But Des would respond: "I hated that film. Why would I want to know what happened to the characters before it started? And anyway, I hate the cinema – the seats are uncomfortable. And it's too expensive. Unless you go on a Monday afternoon…" It was always the case that Des was full of convincing reasons not to do something, whatever it was that Len had suggested. Although really Len should have known better than to call the earlier film "a classic" – with Des that was always red rag to a bull.

The underlying issue, however, as far as Len was concerned, was that it was *always* Len who had to make the suggestions, which Des would often just piss all over as he had with the idea of going to the cinema. In turn this was making Len feel insecure about his height. He was practically a midget and so people used to say that was the real reason he was friends with Des, who was also not very tall (due to being a crocodile). Why couldn't Des ever make the suggestions? And if he wouldn't, couldn't he go along – just once – with a suggestion made by his friend?

The next day, Des suggested that they go down to the playground and chase after some children in the sand. Len was amazed. He was pleased that Des had made a suggestion – he literally couldn't remember the last time – but he was shocked and a bit upset by the nature of it. "But Des," he said, "I don't want to chase children. What about their parents? We'd get in trouble. And I'll end up with sand in my socks and shoes and probably in my pants as well…" He laughed, trying to treat as a joke. He understood that Des was a crocodile and therefore perhaps had different urges, but that wasn't the point – it wasn't like Len had ever asked him to come shopping for tiny clothes or whatever.

But Des just said: "Okay," and turned away in a sulk.

Len felt bad – but what could he do?

The day after that, which was a Saturday, Des crushed Len in his crocodile jaws and ate one of his legs and his head for breakfast. Then he went down to the playground to chase children in the sand and their parents all around the park. He caught and killed two boys and a young mum and seriously injured several others. He had a great time.

But as the subsequent weeks and months went by, Des came to regret eating Len, who had been his only friend and the one human being with whom he'd seen eye to eye (literally). He wished that he had controlled his desire to eat him when Len had shot down his suggestion. He had overreacted. Friendship, after all, was really the only thing in life that made it bearable – unless you were also counting love, which as everyone knew was a much more tenuous and usually temporary arrangement.

COMRADES

There wasn't much to it. You chose the house and waited until it was dark, or at least getting dark, before you descended from the barracks. If you weren't familiar with the terrain you could set off at dusk, you and others, it didn't matter how many went, but most liked to go with at least one other so you could talk about it together after. Not that anyone often talked, by and large we were not very talkative. We knew that we could rely on our comrades, we told ourselves this, but the fact was that we were strangers who had been thrown together by circumstance. And while the passing of weeks and months brought some sense of familiarity, it wasn't based on anything you could explain to someone who wasn't there. *We* were there, that's all it was. But if we'd met elsewhere, even after those weeks and months in the barracks, becoming so to speak familiar, we might not have wanted to talk then either.

Anyway we chose the house. Waiting until it was getting dark before we set out, the majority of the men together. And we made our way down the side of the mountain, winding along paths made by sheep below the jagged lilac sky. No clouds, no moon down in the valley, just the swish and squelch of boots on grass, the slow wail of the hinge. A whispered cursing. Close-by breathing. It's only when it's almost silent that you hear the noise that humans make and begin to wonder at *what it means*... As one by one through the gate we gather at the very edge of the yellow that glows from the house and watch the lives inside.

PARTICLES

These last few weeks, my wife and I have not been getting on. We both retired some years ago and moved to a house in the countryside, away from the hustle-bustle. It brought us tremendous satisfaction. I would not perhaps characterize our life as *happy*, but we were contented – as contented as we had ever been. The accident was a turning point, obviously, but the consequences and repercussions have been worse than I could have ever imagined, and increasingly I'm given to worry that things will never return to the way they were before.

First and foremost, my wife gets tired and is mostly unable to leave her bed. This is a change from how my wife used to be: an energetic, active person, even in her later years. Whereas now she can't even leave the bedroom – and I'm running out of ways to try and address the situation.

"How are you today?" I ask.

"Tired," she says, invariably.

"Any better than yesterday? Did you sleep well?"

"No, Freddie, please don't: can't you see how tired I am? Questions make me tireder. Please, no more questions today. Please, Freddie, no."

But my name isn't Freddie, my name is Eric, and "tireder" isn't a word. I try to explain these things to my wife but she doesn't seem to listen. And I don't want to press her in case it makes her cry again – silently and without tears, as if she were all dried up.

Each night, I dream about the accident.

The tractor is on the hillside, below the oak, and my wife is on top of the tractor trying to prop the stepladder against the trunk, under its lowest branch. Mercury, our cockatoo, is perched on this branch, looking down at my wife with his head to one side, as if incredulous at her behaviour. Meanwhile, standing beneath the tree, I share the surprise of the cockatoo as I stare up at my wife on top of the tractor with a sinking unease that resembles paralysis. The lowest branch is about twenty feet above the ground, about ten feet higher than the figure of my wife silhouetted against the clear blue sky. In my dream, I never get further than this.

The oak, in reality as well as my dream, used to have several lower branches – first at nine feet, then at thirteen, then at sixteen feet and so on – until my wife cut each of them down after each occasion that the bird escaped, to prevent him, theoretically, from escaping again. And it *had* been almost a year since Mercury last flew from the living room window and made his way as far as the oak halfway up the hill. On other occasions he had sat on the windowsill, his head cocked, looking out, but since the last of these branches came down – until the accident – he had not ventured further. This was pleasing to my wife, who would regularly tell me that we could sell the stepladder since from now on we wouldn't be needing it. "The Evergreens need a stepladder. So do the Applejacks. If we offer it to both we can start a bidding war. Mercury will never fly that high. The stepladder is redundant."

But I put the stepladder with the broken cement mixer in the barn, thinking it wasn't a good idea to start another bidding war so soon after everything with the earthenware jug that my wife said she had found buried in the garden.

It was winter the following year when Mercury escaped again, by which time both my wife and I had forgotten all about it. It was not a good day. The weather was bad and my wife was angry – not only about the cockatoo but also about the stepladder, which I hadn't attempted to sell to the neighbours despite her recommendations.

"This one isn't even tall enough to reach the lowest branch," she complained. "If we'd auctioned it off last year, as I said, we could have bought another one. The funds from the auction of the first ladder, managed correctly, would have covered the cost of a second ladder – one with an extension. I expect we would have had enough to buy a new tablecloth as well, if you'd only done as I asked you to…"

"Do you really think it's safe for you up there on the tractor?" I said, "in such a strong wind?"

"Do be quiet," said my wife.

Afterwards we lay in the cold wet grass.

"I'll stay here with you, I promise," I whispered, stroking her hair. "Until you're better, I won't go away – I'm not going to leave you out here on your own…"

Mercury flew down from the branch on the oak and perched on the bonnet of the tractor. "Supper-time! Supper-time!" he squawked and strutted. "Food getting cold – it's supper-time!"

My wife emitted a long slow moan and opened a bloodshot eye.

Then she opened her other eye and looked at me with both. "I think I've broken my neck," she said.

———————

I carried my wife back down the hill and inside the house and upstairs to bed. She wasn't able to answer my questions as to how she was feeling following the accident – but nonetheless I stayed with her, perched on the edge of the mattress, just to reassure myself. The supper that I had prepared for us was getting cold in the oven downstairs, which I'd turned off before we left the house. "It will take ten minutes," I remembered her saying.

Then my wife started muttering under her breath. It was some kind of complaint – she was shaking her head – but by this time the idea of my dinner downstairs was disabling my concentration. It's important that I eat, I kept thinking over and over, until this was the only thought in my head and I felt sure I was going to collapse. So I told my wife that I was going downstairs.

"Shall I bring you some food?" I asked.

"Supper-time! Supper-time!" muttered my wife. "Supper-time! It's on the table!"

I knew that if Mercury ever came back I would not be able to forgive him.

Although it was nearly cold, I had roasted the chicken to perfection, the roast potatoes were crispy and the carrots still had some crunch. Only the broccoli had gone a bit soggy and so at first I didn't eat any. But if my wife was here with me, I found myself thinking, she'd make me eat the broccoli, too – and of course then I felt guilty about it. I ate three pieces of broccoli and threw the rest away. Then I returned upstairs.

"I think it might be for the best if we don't tell anyone. About the accident. We wouldn't want to worry them, now that it's over and done with. You know how sensitive Hugo gets. I don't want everyone coming round and worrying, fussing about. I want it to be just the two of us, like it's always been."

But my wife appeared to have fallen asleep.

I turned out the light, closed the door and went back down for a glass of wine.

I slept in the spare room.

The next morning, my wife told me that she was feeling a great deal better. She agreed it was best that Hugo didn't know, now that it was over and done with, and so I phoned him up to tell him that his mother had gone on holiday. He asked me to where.

"Japan," I said, "For at least a month."

Hugo sounded surprised. "But Dad – what? She never said… What's she doing in Japan?"

"Sushi," I said, "Samurai swords. Karaoke. It's plausible."

Hugo drove here in his Land Rover and started banging on the door. I stood by the fridge where I knew he couldn't see me. After twenty minutes, he left.

Later I phoned him up and told him, "I'm in Blackpool. Your mother's on a sushi tour in Japan, and I'm in Blackpool. Don't come snooping around."

Hugo stayed away until the following morning. I watched his Land Rover from the bedroom window snaking up the track. His progress was unbearably slow, but the mud wasn't nearly deep enough to swallow a vehicle with four-wheel drive and soon the banging and ringing began and I knew that he knew I was there.

I opened the door. We went inside. I filled the kettle and made us tea. His presence made me anxious and I kept on having to clear my throat.

"How was Blackpool?" he asked.

We went upstairs to visit his mother.

"Mum! Oh God: what's happened to you?"

"I broke my neck," my wife said.

We went downstairs to discuss things, father-to-son.

Hugo and his new wife – whose name is not Focaccia – moved into our house the following weekend and began to fill it with their things. They came with Freddie, who is eight years old and Focaccia's son from a previous liaison. His fingerprints are all over the bannisters, and tennis racquets fall out of cupboards whenever you open the doors.

These new conditions have surely contributed to the fact that my memory is failing me, but Hugo's wife is incredibly stubborn – she simply will not compromise. "Hugo," she says. "Your father, please – tell him my name is not Focaccia."

Or else she gets enraged with me: "*I am not Focaccia!*"

Meanwhile Freddie is only at school for a fraction of the working day, as they found something in the water tanks that would eventually have poisoned the children. As a result, from lunchtime onwards I am left on my own with the both of them – and until Hugo gets back from work we have to speak to each other directly.

"Must the boy always be shrieking?" I ask her.

Focaccia attempts to contain her rage. "The boy's name," she says, "is Freddie."

She proceeds to spell it out.

But since this is what my wife now calls me, I have no trouble with Freddie's name. And Freddie it is not a foreign name – "It is therefore, unlike Focaccia, easy to remember. As my wife will testify…" I am forced to comment, walking away.

Then Focaccia washes the dishes and violently mops the floor, cursing me in her furious Latin manner.

I have had to move out from the spare room I had been sleeping in since the accident – the room now belongs to Focaccia and her sisters, photos of whom cover the wall. None of her sisters are remotely attractive and all of them look very unhappy, but they have travelled the world to a remarkable degree, always together and lined up in the same order.

Freddie now sleeps under the stairs where the hoover used to be, which in turn has had to be moved to the barn, next to the ladder and the broken cement mixer.

Nobody seems happy with these new arrangements, least of all my wife, whose condition has certainly not improved as a consequence of so much change. Still unable to leave the room, she is also now barely able to speak. She just sits, eyes not-quite shut, propped-up awkwardly against her pillow as I try my best to talk to her and somehow raise her spirits.

"Do you remember that film we saw?" I asked her today. "The one with the chimpanzee who ran away with all the money?"

"No, Freddie: please don't speak," she murmured. "Freddie, let me sleep."

"But… I'm not…" I began to say.

Then Freddie stampeded into the room, pretending to be a fire engine. He clambered onto the bed and started jumping up and down. "Grandma! Grandma!" he shrieked.

"Freddie!" I shouted, or tried to shout. "Freddie, stop that! No jumping on Grandma!" But I can't even tell if he knows that I'm there or is able to hear me above his shrieking – while my wife seemed to think it was me on the bed, despite the fact that he's shouting "Grandma" as he jumps about all over her.

"No, Freddie, no," she continued to murmur. "Please, don't: I'm so so tired."

I wanted to strangle him.

And sometimes I want to scream at the woman I knew: "How could you let this happen to us? How could you let them move back in? How could you let them change everything and lock us up in this little room? How could *you* change?"

"Let me sleep…" she says.

The bedroom vibrates with the buzzing of flies and every day there are more. Focaccia has told Freddie that he's not to come in but yesterday he opened the door and stood in the corridor and stared at us, before slamming it shut and running for his mother. He was eating some kind of ice lolly so it may be that the seasons are changing, but the windows are shut because of the flies, with the blinds pulled down so my wife can sleep. I wonder if the door has been locked from outside?

My wife no longer murmurs, she crackles and whirs.

Sometimes, when I lie beside her, my head is filled with a kind of noise like listening to a transistor radio that is no longer broadcasting programmes.

It's the flies, I have to remind myself.

It's only the flies.

I don't know how many days went by before I decided we must go downstairs. The flies followed us out of the bedroom – unless they were only following my wife. I tried to carry her beside me as if I were merely helping her to walk, but I wasn't strong enough and we fell to the floor and lay together in the upstairs hallway, just as we had outside in the dew. It was like I was dreaming. The idea of the cold wet grass was beautiful – the icy smell, or absence of smell – and I wanted to roll and push my face deep and down into the mud where Freddie's shrieking couldn't reach me, nor Focaccia's furious clattering, nor the flies, which were worse than anything. They swarmed above us, dive-bombing.

Inside my wife's head, from a filling in her teeth, I could hear the voice of a newscaster. The news was all about Mercury and the places he had visited. The newscaster's voice was from the past. He might have been commentating on the Queen's Coronation and her subsequent tour of the Commonwealth.

Hugo and his family were sitting at the dining table eating some kind of rice that Focaccia must have cooked. Hugo had his back to us, curled forward over his plate, while Focaccia was talking about a woman she had met that day on the bus and had some kind of argument with. So only Freddie was watching as I dragged my wife step by step towards them.

It reminded me of our honeymoon. The scrunching of pebbles beneath our feet and a wild wind blowing us towards the penin-sula – the day that we swam and I caught a chill and had to spend the rest of the week in bed. "Honeymoon Hospital," my wife kept saying, repeating it again and again as she would whenever she came up with a joke. "It's lucky I'm here to keep you alive!"

It had been her idea to swim of course. She was the one who

always had the ideas.

"Mum… Mum… Mum…" said Freddie. I could see the food in his open mouth as he banged the end of his fork on the table harder and louder each time.

"Freddie, shhhh!" said Focaccia crossly, grappling with his fingers to make him hold his fork properly. Then she saw us on the stairs and stopped. "Hugo… Hugo…" she said.

I stood with my wife's cold hand in mine. The flies swirled.

Hugo, without yet turning around, leant forward in order to speak with Focaccia – a strange, small, quiet conference – while Freddie continued to stare at us. The sight of the chewed-up rice in his mouth suddenly made me feel weak and I didn't know how much longer I could stand there waiting for my son.

It was true I had never liked his wife. Perhaps I had not made things easy. But had we not, his loving parents, cared for him for many years long before she was around? And was it not, even now, his parents' roof above his head? – and not just Hugo's but all their heads, Focaccia's and Freddie's *alien heads*…?

Finally he turned around, his head twisted awkwardly over his shoulder, and I saw his dismay, his helplessness. It was as if he knew that he had done something wrong and expected to be reprimanded – and at this moment, instead of resentment, all I felt was a terrible urgency. This was my chance to speak to my son, the last chance I would have.

"Hugo," I croaked – a deathly croak. "Hugo – *listen to me!*"

I tumbled forwards.

Somewhere that I couldn't see, Hugo and his family were sitting in a perfect silence.

I was happy that I was with my wife.

We awoke on the bonfire, side-by-side. Nobody spoke as we set alight and felt ourselves consumed by the blaze. We lay in a comfy heap, watching the world as it twitched and swam, hazy in the purple gloaming. Focaccia and Freddie took Hugo by the hand and led him away down the hill.

We swarmed, flickering – millions of us.

Flames sang as branches whistled.

Oak leaves curled and spat.

IN THE MORNING

The mist. You walk around too long in it, you don't remember which way you came, which way you were going, why. You wait for the mist to clear.

A roadside. A lay-by. A car screams past, I'm jogging after it, it's involuntary, I must be somewhere, I recognize it, it's the same as places I've been before. Exactly the same? Everything is a long way off, like a mechanism is gearing up but hasn't yet made sense of things. A hut up ahead. The Coffee Cabin. The hatch is open, a light is on, a mess of brown sliced onions is sizzling. It's empty. I can hear the whir of the fridge. A bottle of milk on the counter next to a big round bottle of ketchup, red, and a big round bottle of mustard, yellow. Plastic bottle, green label, semi-skimmed, I remember that. I know I had a girlfriend once but that's a long way off as well. A lot of time waiting by the side of the road. A lot of cars, then the early morning sun. That's when I remember things. The rest of it only comes in glimpses, cooked breakfast for Sunday lunch, a mobile phone alarm going off, light coming in at the edge of the blind, rain against the slanting window, the smell of sex in the room. The onions mean there's someone near.

Using the toilet? I never need the toilet now but I like the sound and slosh of milk.

I used to travel a lot, selling. I set off late for my appointment and I got lost on the way. I'm tired of travelling. I've had the time to get used to it and I'm ready for a different challenge. That's what I'll tell them when I get to my appointment. If you'll put your faith in me I'm ready to take the opportunity.

A car screams past in the other direction and I'm jogging again, it's involuntary, when the roads get busier later on I won't have to chase them any more, too many, I'll stand with my arm stretched out and stare as they zip back and forth and sometimes one stops, but not very often, that's why I'm late for my appointment. Most of the time the cars don't stop, it's because of how I look these days, but this one jerks off the road and waits at the end of the lay-by for me to catch up. I've stopped jogging. I used to run along the canal, I'd run all the way to the end of the towpath and up the stone steps to the road. I can't remember why I was running but I'm through with all that travelling now. I walk with my hand up in the sky to block the sun above the trees, it's blue, the car, with it's brake lights on, vibrating with bass from the music inside. I'm alert to things these days, rhythms and resonances, surges in the atmosphere, ebbs, lags, insinuations. I'm at the passenger door. A girl in a mini-skirt sleeps in the back. A man leans across and opens the door, pushing it open so it swings, the music flows out as I step in and the door swings back and shut again. Pupils black like an eclipse, short ginger stubble, a blood-red t-shirt, he clicks down the music, looks at me, grins, looks at the girl in the mini-skirt, puts a finger to his lilac lips and winks. I'm holding a pint of milk in both hands.

"Oi you got a lid for that?" he says. "Don't want that over my upholstery... Only joking fella – this ain't a licensed cab! You ready?" Reversing backwards, he drags the wheel right and right, brakes, wheels screech, the clutch engages, we grip the road and we're away. The lurch of milk in its plastic bottle. No lid, it's at the Coffee Cabin. The girl in the back seat makes a noise, shifts her legs, her skirt scrapes her tights but she doesn't wake up. I can tell these things. Who's asleep, who's pretending. The pressure in their arteries, their secrets, the things they don't even tell themselves. I hear it all. I'll tell them that. I'm ready for something different now, I'm ready to put what I've learnt in the service of a higher purpose. You have to be confident, aspirational, ask questions, I remember that. The rest is hazy, not important. I just need to get to my appointment and show them that I'm well-prepared.

Sunlight, it's involuntary, my hand is up again to block it. The man leans across and pulls down my sun-vizor. I'm close to the stubble down his neck, the sweat dried white on the neck of his t-shirt, his sun-burnt ear, but I can't smell anything, I've lost that now, I can't even smell the time of year.

"Up all night as well?" he says. "Don't worry, I'm safe to drive! I love this fucking time of day… What dance music you into fella? – sorry, I gotta blare this track…" He clicks it louder, bangs the roof, sways the car with his other hand, hums, murmurs, shakes his head, pulls himself close to the steering wheel and then pushes back into his seat. A turbulence in the frequency as a lorry looms and catapults past. Granules congealing in his nostrils. "Yes! I fucking love this tune!" He bangs the roof with his fist again.

"So: where you heading fella?"

"I'm late for my appointment," I say.

He turns and laughs and grins at me. "Yeah, I like it, nice! Don't worry though, it ain't Monday morning just yet…"

I won't be able to hold the milk for long. Small objects, things with holes or handles, but only for short periods of time, if I don't think about it, when it's just in my hand. I can hear the milk and what its feeling. It's oblivious to where it is, its motion and trajectory. All it knows is the temperature and the shape of the inside of the bottle.

The young man thumps his chest with a palm. "You get into that space, you know? You're in the music, right inside it, ah I love that feeling fella – it's… *it's fucking spiritual!*" Each time he thumps a smooth vibration, a surge of breath, a message from the buzzing metal beneath the foam inside my seat. I suppose I like this music too. "Yes oh yes oh yes oh yes oh yes! Now you're moving, now you're with me – careful you don't spill that milk now fella, you get that on my upholstery and I'll have to charge you double…

– just jokes! You keep on moving fella – yeah! – *yeah!*" He howls at the moon. "Oh yeah you've got some groove right there – don't stop! – don't stop 'til you get enough!"

The occasional moments when things are clear. Moments out beyond the mist, of sunlight, on the brink of time.

The girl in the back is now awake. She tenses her shoulders and neck to sit but doesn't open her eyes. She's scared.

"Bonnie, check out the hitch-hiker, I found him by the side of the road on the run with a pint of semi-skimmed! Yo Jacko, this is Bonnie – I kidnapped her from a field…" He winks.

"I'm going to throw up."

"What's that?" He clicks the music down.

"I'm going to throw up."

"Don't fucking throw up in the car!"

We swing to the left at a sudden angle and jolt to standing, another lay-by, the license plate pressing the leaves of the foliage. The milk has sprayed up and through my hand but I'm still managing to hold the bottle, despite the drag of gravity. I start to remember what's going to happen…

"If you're gonna throw up, throw up in the ditch."

"There isn't a ditch…"

"The hedge, whatever! – just don't throw up in the car! Ah shit fella, that milk's gone everywhere! What you got milk for anyway? Why ain't you got a lid for it?"

The girl in her mini-skirt crawls out of the car. Her bra against the edge of the seat, her palms on the grit and the grass, her knees. The man stops the engine. The girl vomits. Milk is splattered across the dashboard, its progress down the moulded plastic a piece of music

I can't remember. I know I used to play the piano. I used to live somewhere. I remember the rain against the window, the warmth and darkness in the loft. The girl's vomit against the leaves, being wiped from her lips along her thumb. Not even a mile away, the woman from the Coffee Cabin clambers back through a gap in a hedge, she was trying to pee but sensed I was there, sometimes they can, they get a feeling, the dew on grass against her thigh, cold and tickling, but she didn't stand up. I had a girlfriend. Ramona, they'd named her after the song. I remember the smell of sex in the room, the idea of it, I remember that, and her last words to me, "You think you're special…" and she smiled at me under the duvet and I left and I never made it back. I got lost on the way to my appointment, in the mist, among the trees. They came and stood in their yellow jackets in the headlights of their flashing trucks and looked at me, I remember that, while others hosed the fire out. Then the heat as tyres gripped and spun and they towed my car away. Then only darkness. Mist.

The milk in the rubber grooves at my feet. Against my back, the patterned fabric, milk sucks through to the foam inside. The girl puts the side of her face in the grass and stares one-eyed at where she's vomited. The man watches her in the wing mirror, a squash of flesh in breathing skin, heart strong, blood pumping. He hasn't noticed the milk in places it wouldn't reach if he was me, there's none of it on my hands, my clothes. At some point suddenly he will. Always suddenly. Then I'm back on my own.

The girl is tired but she's too ill to sleep.

"Ah man, this is fucking nonsense! I should have just banged her back at the field. I don't even know who she is…"

I'm tired but I can't sleep either. I have to get to my appointment and try and explain why I'm late.

A FUNERAL

We're all standing up, and my dad is in the coffin at the front of the chapel. The vicar, or one of his assistants, did say that we could all be seated, but nobody sat, and the ceremony carried on again until he said to stand up again. There are twenty-two people at the funeral, including the vicar and his assistants, who I saw getting dressed into their funeral clothes in the changing rooms across the field. I know they don't live here or work here or anything, as the chapel isn't anything like the other chapel that hasn't been fixed yet since the flooding – it still feels like the old sports hall. They used to keep the badminton nets behind the metal shutter that's now got a big white sheet hanging over it, behind where my mum and my sisters are standing. I remember playing badminton, swishing at the shuttlecock with those spindly rackets, and one time I got so angry that I flung the racket and the edge of it cracked the head of the boy I was supposed to be playing with and I had to go and see Mr Barber.

My mum and my sisters are all looking at me and it makes me feel embarrassed that my uncle Michael is still holding my hand, which he's been holding since we got out of the car. My uncle Michael isn't crying, but I know he loved my dad a lot.

I know that after this is over I'll either be going to live with

Michael or moving to live with my mum and my sisters and my sisters' dad, Anthony, who probably didn't want to come to the funeral because of the time that my dad beat him up.

IN MEMORY OF TOM H

These are some things that were true about me.

I was happy, some of the time.

I always tried to care for people.

I wore boots without laces, from when I was a punk rocker.

I was handsome. I was good at my job.

We had a complicated childhood, my dad was not a very nice man. I had a complicated love-life, different women relied on me.

For many years I drank too much.

My girlfriend left me, I drank too much.

My mother died, I drank too much.

My brothers and sisters tried to help me.

The people who loved me tried to help me.

I tried to care for the people who loved me.

The doctor said I drank too much.

I tried to say what they wanted to hear.

I was ashamed, I couldn't stop.

She found me on my sitting room floor.

At my funeral, they wept for me.

GERANIUMS

Someone has stolen my geraniums. The plant-pot they are in was by the front door. I used to keep a spare key underneath until I decided it wasn't necessary. I never lose my key, no one else needs to get into the house when I'm not around, and anyway I *am* around, I'm either at home or I'm at the shop, which is four minutes walk away. But now the plant-pot has been stolen, along with my geraniums.

There are many people in the town and any one of them could be responsible. I am not well thought of by the neighbours or the wider community. They do not come to my shop and so the business does not make any money. I go to the shop only so as to leave the house, and return to the house so as to leave the shop. The shop is a front, and no one buys it – this is the phrase that is often in my head. But since I own both properties and business rates are low, I can afford to continue with this charade out of lack of imagination as to the alternatives.

Of course I am resented for this by people. I have refused to accept their pity in the nine years since my wife passed away. I was lonely but I could not accept sympathy. I began to hate everyone who wished to help me and I kept this up until they had learned to hate me in return. Then I retreated from my emotions and committed myself to my present routine.

I wonder if the person that has stolen my geraniums is someone who knows all this about me and, in this unusual way, is trying to jolt me out of it.

THE HANG OF IT

I have been alive. For some time now. And I think I've got the hang of it. There is no secret. No special handshake. I do not do as much as before. I was younger. Healthy. And energetic. But I had no routine. No routine at all. I saw my friends. My family. The people I worked with. All the time. I went out to see them. All the time. I experienced a range of emotions. I played a variety of musical instruments. I spoke French. Spanish. And some Portuguese. I went to the cinema. All the time. Read books. Played sports. And went on holiday. All the time. I stayed up dancing. All night. My name was always on the guest list. I was handsome. Friendly with many women. I was in love. Madly. All the time. I had sex. In the park. On the train. Standing up. When there was no space to lie down. I had money. And spent it. All the time. I achieved the goals I set myself. And surpassed myself. Over and over again. But this was all when I was younger. In the past. Before I got the hang of it. I don't do any of these things any more. I stay in. With my cat. My ailments. My 49 inch flat screen TV. And stick to my routine.

ON HOLIDAY IN LA GOMERA

I make the coffee.
You make the coffee.
Eat lunch, smoke cigarettes.

Before we leave, you read the map
we bought from the tourist shop
where the German lady gave me
this paper to write on,
printed in error
by previous customers.

And so we set off up the hill,
in our off-duty English
walking uniforms: the North Face
hiking shoes I bought, the Primark
jazz-hands hat, grey trousers –
you've got shorts and Adidas
running shoes, a sort-of cardigan,
sunglasses – plus in my bag
an emergency cashmere jumper.
Our water runs out quickly.

"It's very steep!" another,
larger German lady tells us,
sitting on a rock, drinking
a carton of orange juice,
her bottle of water strapped to her belly.
(Neither of us would ever ask.)

"This isn't fun," you say,
but I'm enjoying it – pleased
I bought those raisins from the
supermercado. (You eat just one,
to combat dehydration.)
I find it easier to be walking ahead
than behind – but you don't seem
to mind.

We reach the top.
Fields of skeletons
of burnt-out trees, with blackened
stumps of still-green palms,
which you find sad – buried
above ground.

(They used to sweep
and clear the mountains
to stop the fires, but now
they don't.)

I know I have
an anxious mind.
I can't stop analysing
our different ways, our
crude, intricate dynamic…
This quiet private mission creep
of mine – it comes
and goes.

More Germans at every table
on the *teraza* at Bar Montaña,
where they serve lunch –
thank God.

La doña Ifigenia
(who has been written of
in the English and German newspapers
in frames on the walls) has never
used the card machine,
she has to ring her son,
who comes
to help us pay.
("*La auténtica La Gomera
no es la auténtica La Gomera,*"
as her restaurant-rival
down the hill
prefers to put it.)

Heading back,
we follow a path
towards the sun – it crosses
the only winding road three times,
then drops us
steeply over the edge,
down into Los Granados
where we're staying,
just as it's getting dark.

A short negotiation about
buying wine, then back
to where we live these days
to smoke the rest of the
cigarettes.

THE SHORTEST ROUTE
TO THE ICE CREAM VAN

When I was not-well, and my mum would phone me every day because she was worried, and every time was another version of the same conversation, or variation of it, for some reason afterwards I would feel compelled to phone my dad, who was living in Norfolk with Ben, his solicitor, and we would have the same conversation as well, or version of it, although at that point Ben was not his solicitor, not any more, or perhaps in fact he *was* still his solicitor, I don't know since I never asked, I mean asked if Ben was still his solicitor or if he still needed a solicitor, I mean maybe if you're actually *with* a solicitor perhaps you don't need one any more, or perhaps, on the contrary, the world being as it is, I mean being a world in which solicitors are frequently if not constantly necessary for all sorts of things that in a different world, an imaginary world, or a version or variation of our world, or indeed in the world *before* solicitors, which did not, presumably, require solicitors in order to function, progress or exist, a world of children, or dinosaurs, or maybe there's a tribe somewhere, with a film crew maybe but no solicitors, but anyway in the *actual* world in which solicitors are indeed necessary, frequently if not constantly, it could well be that's exactly when you need a solicitor even more, I mean when your solicitor is no longer your solicitor because you've eloped with him all at once to Norfolk and so compromised your relationship, I mean your client-solicitor relationship, as if eloping could somehow be carried out in any way other than all at once, in gradual, cautious, prudent stages, but anyway breaking all your vows, I mean not your vows to your solicitor but your vows to your wife and your children's mother, not that there are additional vows for becoming a parent with someone else, we don't have that mechanism, perhaps we should, but then again it's not as if the vows of marriage, in a world of solicitors, have anything like the meaning that they're strictly speaking supposed to have, but anyway that's another story, what I'm saying is that I never asked him about any of that, I mean my dad, about him and Ben, we never had that conversation so we never moved on to its variation, in fact I had only a slight idea that my dad had eloped with his solicitor, who of course had also until that point been my mum's solicitor as well, my *parents'* solicitor, Ben Waddell, I only knew that he'd gone to Norfolk and with everything else that was going on it was possible for me *not* to think about it, to think about this, despite my thinking about so many things and in such a relentless and rigid way that I was now considered to be not-well, and my mum was phoning me every day because she was worried and wanting to check if I was okay, which she knew I wasn't, but anyway then I would phone my dad, I would feel compelled to phone my dad, who I knew was in Norfolk but I didn't know why and I suppose although I wasn't *thinking about it* I was phoning to check if *he* was okay, I didn't realise it at the time but obviously that's what it was, I was worried about *him*, and my head was so full of information that I suppose *not knowing* what was happening when I thought, in general, that I knew *everything*, and knowing that I didn't know, which is probably why I didn't think about it, I mean think about what was happening with my dad and his solicitor, Ben, in a village two-hundred miles away *in Norfolk*, of course I knew Ben was there but it wasn't clear in what capacity, and so I suppose I *needed to know* without knowing that was what I needed, which of course fits in with the *known unknowns* or the *unknown knowns* and all of that, but anyway that's another story and anyway, while I was phoning my dad, my mum was probably being phoned by my sister, Emily, not daily but often, I suppose at least two or three time a week, and this would have been supposedly in order to check that *she* was okay, I mean my mum, when in fact it turned out at the end of it all that Emily in her happy marriage was really the one who was not okay, along with me, her not-well brother, since Eric, the man to whom Emily was so happily married, according to her, subsequently also eloped and did so in much the same way as my dad or perhaps I mean *in the traditional manner*, abruptly and without being clear or at all precise about the reasons, in fact he was almost frivolous or at least dismissive in terms of these, the reasons he was willing to give and the reasons he wasn't willing to give, or able, perhaps that should be able, he was very tall so it may have been easier, I mean Eric eloping from Emily with a woman named Stephanie I know nothing about, not my dad from my mum with their solicitor, perhaps she was taller, I mean Stephanie, but anyway in these phone conversations between me and my mum when she would phone, then my dad and me when I would phone, after I'd spoken to my mum, and probably also between my mum and Emily in conversations I wasn't part of but in which I imagine the same applied, all of us would say more or less the same things that we always said, perhaps even *exactly the same things*, of course the gist would be the same which was probably inevitable given the context, but so too would the order of phrases, the pauses between them, the rhythms and lurches, our words not spoken, all of this became quickly familiar as if the drama we were performing was *literally* a piece of theatre, or else some kind of strange experiment, not exactly a thought-experiment but like that, only for testing emotions, but of course I mean that the things we said when I was not-well were always the same, not the things that we said the rest of the time when I was *not* not-well, if that makes sense, if you count the time I was *mostly* well as time that I was *not* not-well and therefore, for want of a better word, well, a difficult state of mind to define except perhaps *by the absence of symptoms*, but nonetheless a state of mind I can still enjoy when I'm lucky enough but have simply no way of conceptualizing in the periods of time when I am not, when I'm not-lucky and so not-well, the first of which periods, unaccountably, started when I was twelve years old and carried on for about two years, when I found myself, unaccountably, in possession of a completely new mental apparatus with a range of new and frightening options in terms of the thinking I was suddenly capable of, everything changed in a matter of days, and in fact these options were not really options but rather commands that were issued to me, *by myself to myself* is the best I can say it, and which then, to a more or less total degree, determined not only my thinking but my beliefs and so my behaviours, and indeed not just my behaviours, which might imply doing the same things as before only somehow in a different way, *performing* them differently, when really what was happening was the premiere of *a whole new performance*, a drama for which we hadn't rehearsed, a family drama, and one for which no one other me had been given so much as a storyline, while my grip on this, I mean the storyline, was, to say the least, erratic, of course I was the central character and so insisted that every scene took place with me in it and to my specifications, but I couldn't be relied upon in terms of my character's *motivation*, there was *no continuity*, these specifications or plot details would morph and flip and always *definitively*, as if nothing different had happened before and it was everyone else who had got it wrong, but anyway they said it was normal, at least in the context, I mean the professionals, they said it was normal the trouble starting when I was twelve and my thinking changing so radically it was almost as if I had eloped as well, *myself from myself* and of course from my family, leaving a counterfeit version behind who was like my imaginary Siamese twin, not evil exactly but also on balance *not great* either, the professionals said it was all quite normal, in the *abnormal* context, I mean the context of me requiring professionals to be involved in the first place, and continuing to require them to be involved on a frequent basis, in fact sometimes on a constant basis, it ebbs and flows, and of course this all started long before my dad eloped and then Eric eloped, which was less than two years ago, I mean my dad, then Eric eloping nine months later, but anyway when I was *last* not-well and my mum would phone me every day, she was phoning because she was worried about me and wanting to check that I wasn't doing exactly the sort of thing that *I am doing*, here, now, I realise that, up on the garages above the back gardens on my way to the alleyway that leads to the street that leads to the park that's the quickest, no the most direct, no *the shortest route to the ice cream van…*

I'm doing it, but anyway I know it's different this time, it is.

Do I have any proof of that? No.

But evidence, yes I do have evidence, to go back a bit, when I was not-well, I mean mostly or predominantly or perhaps just more

121

not-well than well, and my mum would phone me to check how I was and if I was okay, which she knew I wasn't, which of course in turn was why she was phoning, the *normal abnormal* and all of that, and afterwards I would phone my dad with a definite sense of being compelled by internal forces I couldn't explain, I suppose emotions, it must have been, but different emotions in combination creating further new emotions which we don't have names for or understand, in fact we don't really understand how even the most basic bits of it work, not that we let that hold us back, but anyway really this calling and checking was just an elaborate piece of theatre we were improvising and ritualising in the hope that it would *solve something*, first and foremost my being not-well but also the rest of it, I mean Ben Waddell, my mum's and my dad's solicitor who was suddenly no longer *their* solicitor, or at least not at all in the same way, *emotionally* in any case, which of course shouldn't have much to do with it when getting involved with professionals but probably in fact it mostly does, I mean the solicitor-client relationship in its ideal form, pre-compromised, since for all I know Ben continues to be both their solicitors and perhaps mine too, as well as my step-father, perhaps not technically, I mean not technically my step-father, I suppose I might need to ask him that if it turns out he *is* still my solicitor, which the first several times I met him there was no doubt at all was what he was since that was the reason he was there, his presence being necessary in order that the world we were in could continue to function and even progress, I mean improve and resolve itself, despite my thinking at that time being very much against this idea or rather this *interpretation*, but anyway he was another professional, another *necessary professional*, and despite the extreme and unavoidable connotations this had for me as part of my being not-well, it's true to say that I liked Ben

Waddell and accepted him as my solicitor and was in fact *happy that he was*, even whilst frequently claiming otherwise…

But anyway that's another story, related yes but it's in the past, I mean the story of Ben Waddell in his role first and foremost as *my solicitor* and not my mum's or my dad's solicitor and his role in everything that came after that, which is also a story I'm not going to tell for the simple reason that I *can't*, it didn't feature in my thinking, it wasn't part of my motivation, *it just didn't fit with the rest of the plot*, and so of course now I'm ashamed to discover that I lack the details to *any stories* apart from my one delusional story, when contrary to all the evidence I was adamant *that I knew everything* and also, in sheer denial of this contrary or conflicting evidence, which so many people were so keen to establish and I was so keen to disregard, *that I was the only one who knew*…

So yes, that's a piece of evidence that I'm *not* not-well like I was before, that I'm *more well than not*, that I'm not delusional, before, if I had left the house and started climbing garden walls, our garden wall and the one after that and the one after that and so on, wall after garden wall, trying to be light on my feet, trampling as little as possible, dancing, stretching on my toes, balancing on flower pots and even chatting to the old lady who was sunbathing three gardens along, she wanted to know what I was doing and when I told her she laughed out loud, saying, "Well, don't let me hold you up!" and in fact it was at the back of her garden that I made it up onto the garages, by way of her trellis, and made it as far as my present position at the end of the garages, on the edge, about to drop down to the alleyway that leads to the street and around the corner and across the next street facing the playground is where the ice cream van is parked, I know it's there, and the girl who works in the ice cream van, with her one blue eye and her smile and her eye-patch on the other eye, I only met her two days ago but I soaked up everything, every detail, and before, when I was still not-well, if my mum phoned up and spoke to me and I told her about it and what I was doing she would straightaway see it as *symptomatic*, I mean as a symptom of me being not-well, and of course she would also expect me to deny it and insist instead on *a different story*, a radically different interpretation, however far-fetched, my imaginary Siamese twin at the crease and batting for justice and righteousness and the ultimate victory of good over evil, the *true untrue*, the *sane insane*, the day when the disbelieved of the world would rise up as one in their delusion *and overcome reality*, I wouldn't have put it like that at the time but that was more or less the feeling, that's how I've been, frequently if not constantly and I hope and pray not permanently, at the times when the plot and the patterning and the aura of what I perceive as reality is too much and too significant, in too many ways, the scale and detail, *the texture of it*, that I have to convey it to those around me and especially to those closest to me, to save them, my mum and my dad and Emily, *to save them in order to save myself*, at these times I wouldn't have phoned my mum for all sorts of contradictory reasons semi-secret from myself, but if she phoned me I would have to tell her like the plug being pulled from a reservoir, the gurgling of my bathtub brain, and my mum would listen, *she always listened*, and then I would have to phone my dad and he would listen, *separately but both of them*, it was only Emily who lost patience in the aftermath of Eric eloping, when the only thing I could focus on was the need to convey and for her to accept the contents of my delusional mind, the epistemology of Mr Rumsfeld and global warming scepticism and traffic lights and the colour green and the *affinity* of the number three to the structure of reality, or rather to how we relate to it, our processing of reality and the way in which this is then part of reality, another part we have to process, and the myriad ways in which we pretend that we base on the ways other people pretend, the people in films, in adverts, on television, and so on and on, these threads all part of a central network of pivotal incidents I had dredged from our past, mine and Emily's, or invented or at least adorned, but anyway a past in which Eric, whether pre- or post-elopement, happened not to feature much, which of course was insensitive, I am insensitive, I mean when I'm delusional I'm very or even completely and utterly insensitive, when my thinking expands to incorporate the entire world and everything in it *except anything that doesn't fit*, I mean fit with my latest interpretation or understanding of this world, not new in fact but a variation, a bacterial proliferation towards an infinitude of variations, which is a lot, and anything that runs counter to this must of course be ignored or revised or deleted, preferably deleted, which of course is what I did to Eric, I ignored the fact that he had eloped and deleted what Emily felt about this, or attempted to but she resisted, and so I was cruel as well as insensitive but anyway that's another story, things are better between us now, and it's also true that Emily is a happier person than she was before, I mean with Eric, despite what she would previously claim, *her* insisting, *her* delusion, and so Eric eloping was for the best, in fact his tallness made everything else a strangely awkward and embarrassing process and I'm pretty sure everyone apart from Emily was also relieved to see him go, which didn't help, they just had better ways of discussing it, or *not* discussing it, better than mine, I mean they had *better ways of pretending* but their ways of pretending were *not a conspiracy*, I see that now, the times they pretended and the times they didn't, with me and with Emily, their not-well children, their ways of pretending didn't make them complicit, for all its faults, its lack of honesty, its obviousness and obliviousness with regard to the complicated facts, I mean the facts of Eric's elopement and my dad's elopement and also mine, my elopement into delusional thinking and *my usurpation of myself* at the hands of my imaginary Siamese twin and everything that followed on from it, the professionals and the court of protection and, thanks to Ben Waddell, my long contested diagnosis of *bipolar disorder* or *hypomania* or the much more frightening and exciting *schizoaffective disorder* or even, perhaps most exciting of all but not without the definite taint of being simply *a clinically not-nice person*, I mean a common or garden shit, a *personality disorder* of a diagnosable but uncategorizable kind, once more unto the *known unknown*, the *precise imprecise*, the *medical maybe*, the essential criterion being that *the way you think, feel and behave causes you or others significant problems in daily life*, and *across different aspects of your life*, and when these problems *continue for a long time*, about which my dad often liked to say, "So it's having a personality that's the disorder then?" and my mum said something that I'll never forget, she said, "Well, Paul, I know that they're the professionals and I'm just the nag who gave birth to you, but I want you to know that that's just bullshit, you're not a problem, you're wonderful, you're my wonderful, wonderful son…" and also, this was later on, after he had eloped to Norfolk for whatever the various and complicated reasons I could never find the words to ask him about, my dad said, "Your mum can be argumentative – but most of the time it's because she's right."

So maybe that would be a piece of evidence, solid evidence, I don't know why, maybe if I was to phone my mum instead of waiting for her to phone me, half waiting/hoping, half waiting/ fearing, to resume the familiar family drama, if I was to take the first step and phone her and tell her what was happening, I mean tell her that I was on the garages above the alley and behind the gardens on my way to the girl in the ice cream van whom I knew in the middle of the night last night that I had to see *as soon as possible*, the next day, now, in the autumn sunshine, if I phoned her up and told her *that* and we didn't have the same variation or version of that same conversation, the one where I tell her what I'm doing, the absolute everything of what I'm doing and why I'm doing it and what I'm thinking, and as I tell her, despite my enthusiasm, I start to feel a sense of dread in my recognition that once again, not despite but *because of my enthusiasm*, we're having *the exact same conversation*, the rhythms and pauses, the intonations, we're performing our family drama and the more that I try to make it different the more I make it exactly the same, the intakes of breath, the patterning, the same unmistakable, fatal aura, whatever I did and whatever I do I may be repeating the exact same steps from the exact same farcical blind man's waltz to the edge of the exact same precipice, stretching, dancing, pirouetting, towards the exact same shamefully helpless, devastating anticlimax…

"Paul?" says my mum. "Are you okay?"

"Yes," I say. "I'm really good. I mean, I know I've said that before, but this time I'm really…"

"Paul?" says my mum. "Are you…? Where are you?"

"I'm up on the garage. I climbed through the gardens and I'm up on the garage."

She's worried of course, she has to be.

"The garages? Why are you up on the garages?"

"Because," and I hear how this sounds to her, "it's the shortest route to the ice cream van… But honestly, Mum, it's okay. You don't have to worry, I know what I'm doing. I just wanted to get

127

there the shortest way so I needed to get to the alley."

"Paul, I… Just wait a minute, Paul… *The ice cream van?*"

"Yeah. I'm going to get an ice cream."

"Okay. But Paul… Have you taken your medication?"

"It's okay, Mum, honestly. It's not really about the ice cream. I went there on Sunday when you were at Mike's and I started talking to the girl who works there. And she's nice, I mean she's really nice, and I wanted… I know that it probably sounds stupid but I wanted to make some kind of statement, and I wanted to get there the shortest route…"

"You were talking to the girl at the ice cream van?"

"Yes," I say. "I went for an ice cream. I don't know why. And I started talking to her. I'd never seen a girl with an eye-patch before and so I was asking her about her eye-patch. I wasn't being rude, I was just asking and she thought it was funny, I mean funny that I just asked her without worrying about if that was okay. And so then I was telling her about, you know…"

"About Mr Rumsfeld?"

"Yeah, all of that. The Pentagon…"

My mum laughs. But she's thinking again. Her thinking, my thinking, the lurches and pauses, the intonations, the words not spoken. "A girl with an eye-patch at the ice cream van…?"

"Mum," I say, "you keep on asking me questions like you do when you're worried that I'm not okay. But that's not what this is, I promise. She wears an eye-patch because she damaged it when she was younger, in a cookery class. She put too much mushroom soup in a blender and it exploded and she got boiling hot soup in her eye. I thought she was joking. I thought it must be a dare or a joke or some sort of fashion thing, because she's really pretty, you know, she's beautiful, and so I don't know… I just thought that a girl like that wouldn't have an eye-patch except for a joke. I know that's stupid. But then these kids came up and they were asking her the same thing, like, "Tell us what's wrong with your eye?" And when she told them they didn't believe her and they kept on saying she had to show them or they wouldn't believe her, they kept on saying it, and suddenly she pulled it off and leant right over the counter at them and they ran away screaming. It was really funny… I mean I know it's ridiculous to tell someone something was really funny, but it was… It's her uncle's ice cream van. It's her uncle's but he's had a stroke."

My mum is thinking. But it's not the same.

"Is it nasty, then?" she asks.

"What? Her eye? Yeah, it's horrible! That's why she wears an eye-patch…"

"Oh, right," says my mum. "Okay. So…?"

"I just need to get down off the garages and I can cut along the alley. It's the shortest route and I don't know, I thought if I came this way and if she was there then I might… ask her out…?"

Is this *really* different? The aura, the patterning? The headlong leaps of logic and the frenzy of associations, my thinking always one step ahead of me, leading the dance, the waltz, my moth's flight towards the brightest flame, my spaceship burning up in orbit, I know the steps, I know the precipice, I know, at least I ought to know, I ought to know better, *do I know?*

"Well," says my mum, "thanks for ringing."

"I wanted to ring you and let you know. You honestly don't have to worry."

"Well, I am *a bit* worried. Are you up high?"

"It's quite high, yeah, but it's okay. There's some bins I can drop down onto first…"

"Couldn't you have gone along the street? Wouldn't that have been shorter?"

"But Mum, that's just the quickest route, not the shortest."

"Oh," says my mum. "Well okay, Wittgenstein. Good luck with Pirate Jenny."

"Ha ha ha," I say. "That isn't funny."

"Well," says my mum, "it *might* be funny. Under normal circumstances. But since you're the master of ceremonies, I suppose I'll leave that up to you…"

So that went okay.

I get down from the garage onto the bins and into the alley and now I'm wondering what's going to happen when I get to the park and the ice cream van and the girl with the eye-patch, what will she think, what will I see and know she's thinking as she watches me walking straight towards her, this crazy man with a crazy idea, visibly crazy, who thinks that because he climbed garden walls and over garages and onto bins and along the alley that *this means something*, something new and exciting and frightening and *significant* that he must convey, and convey in such a way that she sees that he's *not* crazy, he's *not* not-well, he's a messenger with an important message, a message not everyone can see but that doesn't mean it's delusional, it's not about how many eyes you've got, two eyes, one eye, three eyes, none, it's about your brain and your way of thinking, it's about *belief*, and it's only one girl that needs to see it and see it's not crazy, or just not care, it's a message and a mission statement and it's not delusional *if she feels the same*, or maybe it is but it doesn't matter, it's a new piece of theatre, an improvisation, but also the oldest, the archetypal, *the intrinsic delusion of the human condition* in all its versions and variations, I mean *it's symptomatic*, and

130

suddenly and all at once and because this is one of those moments in life when everything makes sense *but I'm okay*, I'm *not* not-well, my phone rings again and the person phoning is not my mum having had time to think and changed her mind and decided, *because she has no choice*, to call in the professionals to come and assess me and to take me away, instead it's my dad, phoning from Norfolk, and phoning, presumably, with terrible news, I don't know what news or just how terrible but why else would *my dad* be phoning?

"Dad?" I say. "Are you okay?"

"Yes," he says. He sounds surprised. "Are you?"

"Yeah, I'm good," I say. "I'm going to get an ice cream."

"Is it hot there?" says my dad, incredulous.

"Yeah, it's… What's it like where you are?"

"Well, it's been raining for several days, but we're not yet underwater…"

"Oh right. And how's er… your solicitor?"

"Ben?" says my dad. "Yes, he's okay too. Well, his mum's not well. And he says we should move to somewhere bigger. But I think we're sort of getting used to it…"

"Used to what?" I ask, none the wiser. "Used to Norfolk?"

"Well, yes…" He thinks about it. "Used to Norfolk."

HOW IT WENT

They went walking they went sailing they went dancing they went to the cinema to theatre they went to the theatre only once it's true but they went and he said well and she said yes and they had some other things that they felt about it and that was plenty they went for dinner and she said but and he said yes and for much of the time they couldn't remember what it was they said what they were saying they were together and laughing tingling they couldn't eat they vomited at least they felt like this this queasy butterflies blood in the veins and their eyes were a tingle and they paid the bill and couldn't remember what they'd had it wasn't important in fifty years would the robots care what two people ate for dinner one night − they might! they might! − and falling giddy they gurgled grinned they didn't know what they were laughing at there wasn't a logical reason for it they were stupid with love the thrill of it and they told the man at the table next to them they were going to marry they were going away to Argentina New York to France to anywhere they wanted to to places and over the years they did they did but I won't be telling of that just now just this go get your own tall story and best of luck it's partly luck not wholly and no they didn't get married no but yes they're still together yes and I heard they had a child…

Lightning Source UK Ltd.
Milton Keynes UK
UKHW02f1855130618
324202UK00006B/22/P